Black Waves in Cardiff Bay

John Freeman
(editor)

Cinnamon Press

Published by Cinnamon Press
Meirion House
Glan yr afon
Tanygrisiau
Blaenau Ffestiniog
Gwynedd LL41 3SU
www.cinnamonpress.com

The right of the contributors Paul Belanger, Ruth Calway, Gavin Goodwin, Robert D Leis, Alaleh Mohajerani, Claire Morton, William Muir, Rahul Sethi, Cathy Smith, John Whittles, Nia Wyn, to be identified as the authors of this work has been asserted by them in accordance with the Copyright, Designs and Patent Act, 1988. © 2008

ISBN 978-1-905614-97-4

British Library Cataloguing in Publication Data. A CIP record for this book can be obtained from the British Library

All rights reserved. No part of this publication may be reproduced, stored in a retrieval system, or transmitted in any form or by any means, electronic, mechanical, photocopying, recording or otherwise without the prior written permission of the publishers. This book may not be lent, hired out, resold or otherwise disposed of by way of trade in any form of binding or cover other than that in which it is published without the prior consent of the publishers.

Designed and typeset in Palatino & Garamond by Cinnamon Press

Cover design by Mike Fortune-Wood from original artwork: Cardiff Bay 1 by David Winwood, supplied by agency: dreamstime.com

Contents

Foreword	John Freeman	4
Paul Belanger	Lucky Luke	7
Ruth T Calway	A Progressive County	20
	Not a Plot At All	22
Gavin Goodwin	Poems in Verse and Prose	33
Robert D Leis	Daisy and the Black Squirrel	41
	Icarus in Flight	45
	Three Poems	46
	From *Seran Vale*	48
Alaleh Mohajerani	From *Niku*	53
Claire Morton	From *The Toadstone*	66
William Muir	Little Death	76
Rahul Sethi	Maksuda	87
	Mother	88
	Bara Bazaar	90
	Shit-Water	91
	Twisted Ankle	95
Cathy Smith	From *Shifting Sands*	100
	Gloves	104
	An Ayrshire Cemetery	109
John Whittles	Medicine	110
Nia Wyn	Trauma and the Creative Process	116
Notes on Contributors		127

Foreword

This book is an anthology of writing by the eleven students taking the MA course entitled 'The Teaching and Practice of Creative Writing' at Cardiff University in the academic year 2007-2008. I want to put the word 'student' in inverted commas, though technically they are not needed, because the majority of these 'students' are mature, seasoned individuals with a great deal of varied experience, and they have all, from the youngest to the oldest in the group, taught as much as they have learned during the year.

The anthology consists mostly of their stories, excerpts from novels in progress, and poems. This work has been submitted as part of one or other of the two portfolios of creative writing on which 'students' are assessed. They are also required to write two essays, one about the creative process in relation to writing, and the other about teaching creative writing. One of the contributions to this volume is an essay on the creative process. Alphabetical order of contributors has positioned it at the end of the book, and it makes, I think, a fitting conclusion to a show-case of work which was not only written but reflected on, discussed, and tirelessly re-edited during the year; a year, too, in which systematic thought about writing, and about teaching writing, has been integral to the experience we have shared.

This MA programme has been running at Cardiff for a number of years but this is the first time it has published an anthology like this. What was different this year? The recent arrival of Cinnamon Press has transformed the publishing scene in Wales, for one thing. For another, we had one student, the successful novelist William Muir—Billy to his friends and victims—who refused to stop pushing and nagging us into it. He it was finally who approached Cinnamon, and we are very grateful that Cinnamon said yes.

For the contributors to this volume it will remain as a memento of an exceptional year, and that goes for me too, the editor and course convenor. Behind the words on the page for us lie countless hours of workshops, lectures, discussions, teaching practice, and one-to-one tutorials; public readings by visiting writers and open mic sessions for the course participants; a residential weekend at Gregynog, the university conference centre in mid-Wales; a few evenings out together, and for some, a regular game of frisbee. There is nothing quite like the camaraderie that develops through all this.

On any successful course of this kind the participants learn as much from each other as from anyone, but the teaching staff and visiting writers have been warmly appreciated also. There have been too many visiting writers to name them all; but in addition to my colleagues Shelagh Weeks and Tim Rhys, who with me have carried the course from day to day and week to week, with the indispensable support of Martin Coyle, chair of the Board of Studies, I know the participants would want me to mention the novelist Lindsay Clarke, whose lectures, workshops and regular tutorials have made him as much a part of the year's success as anybody.

To readers who have had nothing to do with all this, and wonder how it may concern them, I would say that this has been an inspiring year for everyone involved, and some of its magic has rubbed off on the writing collected here. It would be wrong to single out individual contributions, and futile to try to characterise each of them. I can only say that I believe the writing here will surprise and delight readers by the very high standard of its achievement, its enormous variety, and its engrossing and enjoyable qualities; and that it can hold its own with any anthology of new writing you care to mention. See if you don't think so when you have read it all.

John Freeman
November 2008

Paul Belanger
Lucky Luke

'We're gonna hide it,' Tom said.

'And draw a map,' Travis added, standing on tiptoe so that Sam would notice. 'I put my magnifying glass and some of those blue flowers by the road in. See?'

Sam threw the tennis ball he was holding and his dog, Luke, tore after it. Taking the lunchbox from his brothers he flipped the latch.

'They're gonna die, aren't they Sam, those flowers?' Tom said. The flowers, tied with string, were already bruised from banging around inside the box.

'Probably.'

Besides the thick and knobby stems there was a rubber-banded stack of baseball cards, a bullet on a keychain, and a buffalo nickel, its contours exaggerated beneath the magnifying glass.

'The nickel's from Mom. She gave us the idea. Pretty cool, huh?'

Sam dug the coin out and handed the box back to Tom. He'd seen buffalo nickels or Indian heads, but never in such good condition. He turned it back and forth, watching light flash first off the buffalo's broad back and then the feathers tied in the native's hair. It seemed unreal without the tarnished rub of being spent and pocketed, and Sam was both wary and enchanted.

'What're you putting in, Sam?' Travis asked. 'It's supposed to be something special. Something you'll come back for.'

Sam smiled at his youngest brother and handed the nickel to him. 'I don't know, Trav, I don't really have anything.' He reached into his pocket and pulled out a few tootsie-roll wrappers for effect. They fluttered to the ground as he took the last deformed candy from the pile and extended it towards his brothers.

'No, Sam. Like your knife or your belt or a drawing; something like Mom's Indian head. She said it reminds her of us,' Tom explained as Travis began a whooping war dance around them. 'And I put my bullet in because I won't be able to shoot my gun in the city. Even if it is only a BB gun.' Luke returned and dropped his ball, unable to resist joining Travis's tribal display.

'Well, I don't have anything for it then,' Sam said, raising his voice to be heard above them. 'Besides, shouldn't you be helping Mom?'

'Shouldn't you be loading the trailer?'

'Nope. Me and Greg are pretty much done here,' Sam said, scratching the back of his sunburned and flaking neck.

'There are still lots of boxes,' Tom said and pointed through the open door of their walkout basement.

'Yeah, but we got all the big stuff already. Greg said he could do the rest.'

'Well, Mom told us to go play. She gave us the idea for the treasure box, remember?' Tom said.

Travis stopped his circular cavort but Luke continued to attack his shoes. 'Yeah, she has a headache,' he said. 'Says she doesn't need us in there right now. I think she's mad.'

Sam whistled, and the dog dropped to attention. 'Ball,' he said, and Luke tumbled over himself retrieving it. Taking it from his mouth, Sam pump-faked it towards the road. Luke gave chase. 'She hates it, too, you know. No one likes it.'

Tom squinted and cocked his head before saying, 'But what're you putting in? We need you. Mom said everyone.'

'Greg, too?'

'Nah,' Travis shook his head, 'just us.'

'Fine,' Sam said and held out the faded and sodden tennis ball. Tom accepted it into the box and both younger boys peered in to see how the new addition looked, how it filled the box.

Sam knew that whatever they tucked under the floorboards or in one of the nooks and chinks of their fort, an old converted shed, would be lost. And though he might not have believed in their treasure map he didn't scoff or tell them to grow up either. 'Make sure you hide it good,' he said. 'You don't want anyone stealing it now.'

Sam prided himself on knowing all of his brothers' hiding places and, as expected, they took off for their fort. He smiled and went in, leaving Luke to continue hunting along the ditch where Travis's flowers grew.

Inside, he helped his Mom make peanut butter and honey sandwiches. She spread the peanut butter and Sam drizzled honey until it started to spill over the crusts. When they had stuffed almost a whole loaf's worth back into the empty bread bag, much more than they needed, his Mom stopped in mid-spread and said, 'Oh, what am I doing?' She sighed and her face, never made up but always beautiful, sagged. Scraping the knife against the rim of the peanut butter jar she asked, 'Where's Luke?'

'I don't know. With Tom and Travis?'

She pressed her lips into a thought and said, 'You know there is a big field across from the new house.'

Sam opened an empty drawer and looked inside. Then he did the same to the two below.

'And the house has a huge basement, just like the one in Belleview. You can have your bedroom down there if you want. You'd have it all to yourself.'

The corners of Sam's mouth were the only thing to smile and he did his best to look at her, but neither the look nor the smile lasted more than a second. 'You need anything else?' he asked, twisting the bag of sandwiches until all the air was forced out.

'No. Why don't you go see what your brothers are up to and play with Luke before we go? Greg will want to leave soon.'

'Can I bring some wood?'

'What for?' Mom asked.

'Well, Luke'll need a place to sleep at the new house, won't he?'

Mom turned to the sink and slid the knife into a shallow pool of soapy water. Rainbowed bubbles grew and popped as she swished a rag through the sink. Sam set the bag on the counter and the end twirled loose, inhaling. Outside, a box broke open in Greg's hands and spilt nondescript black video tapes with handwritten labels unto the gravel. His brothers fought in their fort.

Mom turned and wiped at the counter, making sure it was as clean as the day it was new. She was always particular about how they left a house. It had to be impeccably spotless, as if it was how she'd be remembered.

'Well, can I?'

'Just make sure you play with Luke,' she said and took his head in her hands and kissed it, her nose buried in his hair. She held him there long enough to get a wriggle and, smoothing her shirt continued, 'Greg doesn't want him jumping around the car.'

'He'll be good.'

Mom gave her "I know you know better" look, a look he rarely got anymore, and said, 'He's loud, Sam, and hyper. Not a city dog.'

Sam recognized the look but wasn't sure what she thought he knew. Luke was a good dog. He'd need a kennel. And Greg could go to hell. 'Don't worry about that, Mom. Luke's real quick. I'll take care of him.'

Mom turned back to the sink and twisted the tap. The rush of water resonated with her hushed response. 'Okay. Just go play with your dog.'

Sam passed Greg picking the tapes off the driveway and stacking them back into their dilapidated box. His face was unpleasant and Sam tried to avoid it as he passed, but he was stopped and asked what he was doing.

Luke could be heard harassing the brothers in the shed and it took Sam a second to answer. 'Taking care of my dog, that's what,' he snapped. 'Mom told me to go play with him so he doesn't *annoy* you.'

Greg grunted, standing. The box of home videos, most of which were filmed a lifetime ago, sagged in his hands. 'That's what's wrong with you boys. She's too lenient; babies you still.'

'You should tape that,' Sam said, referring to the box.

'It's fine,' Greg said. 'It's not like you watch them anyhow. I don't know why we're even bothering.'

'You wouldn't,' Sam said, and the door to the shed slammed open as Tom chased Travis with something in his outstretched hand. Luke trailed behind, his bark louder. 'You're an idiot,' Sam said and ran to join his brothers.

'You better say goodbye,' Greg hollered after him.

Travis had scrambled to the top of the embankment near their fort and Tom was at the bottom taunting him with a dead bird. 'Leave me alone,' Travis squealed.

'I'm gonna make you eat it. Now, where'd you put it?'

'I'm telling Mom.'

Sam was nearly a head taller than Tom and in full possession of his rights and duties as the oldest brother. 'Wow, Tom,' he said, 'did you shoot that?'

'I wish. Luke found it, but Travis hid the box while I was trying to get the darned bird from him. Now he won't tell me where he hid it.'

'I didn't say that. I said I won't show you.'

'You're dead,' Tom said.

'Mom,' Travis screamed, and they both bolted for the house. Luke tensed, but didn't follow after them, and Sam knelt to give his dog a good scratch behind the ear.

'You're getting a new house too, boy. And I'm going to build you the best one ever,' Sam said, dodging licks and paws. 'You have to be good though, okay?' Sam held Luke's ears back so the dog had to look at him. 'And quiet. We'll have lots of neighbors at the new place.'

Luke wrestled away and ran into their fort. All of the windows except the one in the loft were boarded up and this cast the converted shed in a dim, dusty light. Sam followed Luke and plunked himself into the ripped and stinking recliner they had salvaged from the house when they had first moved in. They usually left their forts intact because that's how they'd like to find one, and all of their posters and road signs were still nailed to the walls. Sam snapped a wick off one of the stumpy candles next to him and rolled the sooty black between his fingers and then into his jeans.

'Well, boy, what do you think?' he asked. 'You ready?' Luke lay on his hip and licked himself. Then Sam had an idea and asked, 'Should we move that box on Travis. You know he can't keep a secret. He'll tell Tom soon enough, anyway.' The mischief lit up behind his eyes and Luke stopped his grooming, listening.

Sam went and peeked through a hole in the boarded up window. His brothers had been waylaid by Greg and were hauling his weights to the nearly full trailer. He pictured his real Dad teaching him how to saw boards and drive nails, the twisted knots of his forearms and his guiding hands. It was one of the memories his brothers didn't have and one of the many reasons it was easier for them to get along with their stepfather.

'Do you remember your first house? The green one?' he asked, and Luke did. 'It took us three weeks to build. Trav was just born then.'

Luke barked.

An old, graffiti-ed cable spool filled a corner of their hideout. Sam rolled it aside and knelt. There were two loose boards and he used a knothole to take out first one and then the other. Underneath was a well-formed hole and a mason jar, but no lunchbox. Sam shook the jar but it was empty. Travis used to keep his money in it, and though there had never been more than a buck and a half in it, it had always been safe with Sam.

'It should be here,' he said and Luke stuck his nose in, double-checking Sam's conclusion, but the box was certainly not there.

His brothers started calling his name as they approached the fort. He quickly replaced the jar and re-covered the hole. They were almost upon him by the time he got everything back in place and he made himself look busy tying a shoe. Luke trotted out to meet the brothers.

'Sam. We're gonna go pretty soon,' Tom said, delivering their mom's message, 'Make sure you have everything.'

'And don't forget to whiz,' Travis said, making the universal sign for pissing.

'I need to get some wood for Luke's new doghouse,' Sam said to Travis before glancing from his brother to the spool in the corner and back again.

'Take the window,' Tom said, passing between his older and younger brothers. Then, with a long drawn, high-pitched 'O!' and a crane kick Tom sent the piece of plywood that covered the window flying. Several small birds were startled from the tall weeds beneath. Light poured in, and Sam had to shield his eyes, breaking his stare with his brother. Luke yapped and chased after the birds outside.

When his eyes adjusted Sam gave Travis the slightest of nods and smiled. Travis relaxed and said, 'You'll need some nails too.' He climbed into the loft to get the jar of nails. 'Do you want this chair cushion? It could be a bed,' he said from up top.

Tom was yanking on part of the window, trying to bend and pry the nails loose.

'Sure, Trav,' Sam said, 'And Tom, isn't there still some stuff left from when we did the roof?'

'I'll go look,' he said, the window sill hanging on by twisted nails.

The three of them got everything they'd need for Luke's house and piled it neatly by the trailer, but the door was padlocked.

A loud 'What the hell!' came from the other side of the trailer and then, 'Your damned dog's got that bird again. Son of a bitch.'

'Get the key from Mom,' Sam said, placing a hand on each of their shoulders. Get everything loaded and I'll take care of Luke.'

'Greg's probably got the key,' Tom said.

'Talk to Mom.'

The three of them walked around the trailer together and before Greg could say anything about how he needed to watch his dog or how they all needed to listen better, Sam was off, whistling after Luke.

'Hey, Greg,' Tom said, 'can we get into the trailer?'

Luke waited for Sam to catch up, and when Sam came near he ran off again. It was a game he used to play when he was learning fetch. Luke would only drop one ball if Sam threw another. He'd trade the bird for a ball now; Sam was sure of it. He stopped, reached into his pocket, and pulling out a fist said, 'Luke. Luke-boy. Fetch.'

He made as if to pitch the ball high over the dog's head and Luke followed the imaginary arc. The bird, hanging and flapping from the side of Luke's mouth as though still alive, was let go in full stride and tumbled to a stop in the yard. Sam kicked it under a bush and whistled again. Luke returned panting, unaware he'd lost anything.

Mom was outside then, talking to Greg who had changed places with her indoors. She handed Sam a leash as he and Luke approached. 'We're just about ready. Make sure you don't lose him. I don't want him running off now.'

Sam hooked the leash to Luke's collar and went to sit by his brothers who had now stationed themselves on the lawn at the edge of the drive. August corn shone in the field across the road, and Sam fastened his eyes on the same place as theirs, past the creek that ran behind it, and past the small wood beyond that. They looked to the very edge of their world with part hopeful adventure and part sorrow.

'There's a field across from the new house,' Sam said.

Tom and Travis looked up to him, his face clear, cowlick sticking out. Luke sat at his side, still.

Mom and Greg could be heard arguing inside, but the boys ignored it as background noise. Looking down at his brothers, Sam smiled and said, 'Mom gave me the basement.' A general 'no fair' came from the boys and Sam continued, 'I thought we could put a fort down there.' Dissent quickly turned to disbelief. 'Sure. The basement will be plenty big.'

The argument moved outside.

'For crying out loud, Greg. Don't be such an idiot.'

'Sooner or later,' he said, following behind with the last of the boxes.

'Can't you just leave it be?'

'It's not fair, Lynn.'

'What the hell do you want?' their mom asked, turning on him and flapping a pair of yellow rubber gloves in his face. 'It's hard enough.'

'For God's sake, woman.'

'They're mine.'

Luke pulled on his leash and barked at the quarrelsome adults.

'Tell them.'

Mom threw her gloves into the box in Greg's arms and told the boys to get in the car. She opened the back door for them and waited. Luke yapped, but the boys remained still and silent. Greg awkwardly propped the box on his knee and closed the house door for the last time. Sam thought he had learned all there was to know about leaving but still winced at the familiar hollow thud.

'Come on, boys.'

Greg carried the box, a dilapidated miscellany of things nearly left behind, and added it to the trunk. He brought the trunk down with a swish and it bounced back against the BB gun jutting out of the box. Sam thought to tell Greg to be careful, but stooped to calm Luke instead.

Surprisingly, their stepfather didn't yell. He merely grunted and moved the gun. 'Listen to your mother,' he said from inside the trunk.

One by one the boys' hair was tousled as they climbed in through the door. The other door was broken. It didn't open and the window didn't go down. Tom complained about having to sit there.

'Well, your brother has the dog so you'll just have to deal with it,' Mom said, and swung the door closed.

Travis looked ridiculously small between his brothers, almost as ridiculous as the smile he gave each of them. Tom looked over and punched him in the shoulder. Tears welled immediately and the crying came later. The trunk closed. Mom and Greg ignored Travis's wailing and continued to bicker. Luke added his voice to the cacophony in the car and Sam had to hold his snout to get him to shut up. Tom tried the same technique with Travis.

Justifying the torture, Tom whispered into his ear, 'Where is it, barf-face? Where's the box?'

Travis bit him and crowded closer to Sam.

'Cut it out, Tom,' Sam commanded.

'I'm not telling,' Travis said, emboldened by his brother's support. 'You'll never find it without me. And I'm not telling.'

Tom shoved Travis's head once more as Mom climbed into the car. She situated a paper bag between her legs, looked behind her, and told all three of them to buckle. Their obedience was quick, if disorderly. Luke's butt twitched in the excitement and Mom let him climb over the seats. She spoke to him in her animal voice, the same she used with the birds and the coon out back, the same Sam remembered her using with Travis.

'So, did you hide it?' she said, letting Luke slide back onto Sam's lap and putting her own belt on. Outside, Greg lit a cigarette and looked at the family packed into the car.

'Yep,' Travis said. Unlike Travis, Tom wasn't one to tattle and zipped up when she asked him where it was. 'It's a secret,' Travis answered for him.

'That's nice,' she said. 'Did everyone pee?'

Their nods left little room for conversation. Mom continued looking back for some time before finally straightening her body. Greg flicked his cigarette in the direction of the burn barrel and spat.

Unused to the weight of the trailer the car jerked and the gravel under the tires grated louder. 'Here goes,' Greg said, leaning forward as if their things were hitched to his back rather than the car. 'All aboard.'

'You ready?' Mom asked, but the three of them were watching out the window, trying to get a last view of their home beyond the giant white trailer. Travis leaned over Tom in order to see and Tom resisted harassing him. They simultaneously registered the pile of wood, hardly noticeable but for the blue and yellow cushion, at the side of the drive.

'You forgot the wood?' Sam said, reaching over and punching Tom in the shoulder. 'I told you to get that stuff in the trailer.'

The shoulder bruised, and so did his pride. 'I did,' Tom whined, 'Greg put it in. He wasn't going to, but Mom made him.'

'Well, he didn't,' Sam said.

Greg was already looking in the mirror by the time Sam redirected his glare. His brown eyes were softer than normal, though Sam wouldn't have noticed, and he turned away. 'Sorry, boy.'

Mom tuned the radio to a crackling oldies station and the adults drove facing forward, the children sideways. Luke held his head high out the window, the nauseating freshness of manure sweeping through the car. Over the bridge they fished under, past the foundation of the burnt-down building, and down the long straight haul through farm after glorious farm, Sam's brothers retraced the year it had taken them to map out their insignificant corner of the world.

But Sam didn't say goodbye to the fields and wooded hillocks and dells. Rather, he discarded Greg's apology out of hand and kept his evil eye leveled on the mirror as the friction of the road, rubber humming and bumping along the tractor-cracked asphalt, echoed between his temples. 'You know,' his stepfather said, looking up again, 'I don't use the rearview when I'm pulling a trailer.'

'Idiot,' Sam said and aligned himself with Luke to whisper in his ear, 'Sorry, boy, we'll figure something out.'

'Maybe you can use the toy box,' Tom suggested.

'Yeah, cut a hole in it. And...'

'You're not cutting up your toy box,' Mom said, snapping her attention on them. 'Just leave it be, Travis.'

'It was my idea,' Tom said.

Mom went back to the radio and fiddled with the dial, but rather than clearing up, the static worsened and she couldn't get it back to where it had been. Sam and Luke ignored them all, their heads close, exchanging whispers.

The radio was turned off in frustration and the family drove on in silence. It was almost an hour into town and would take another five after that to get to their new house. When they got into town, Travis told Mom that he had to pee again and so they passed the Gas Shack, where gas was always a penny cheaper but there was no bathroom, and filled up at the Shell station instead. Greg popped the door to the gas tank, leaned against the trailer and started calculating miles as the cost cycled higher. Tom and Travis ran inside to get the bathroom key.

'I can't believe those boys,' Mom turned around and said once Sam and Luke were back inside. Luke paced the seat and spun around several times looking for a place to sit. Sam remained quiet long enough for Mom to turn back and leave him alone.

'So why didn't you take my stuff?' The boy pinched his dog's ear and the dog bit gingerly at his fingers. He leaned between the seats and put his hand on her arm, 'Mom?'

'There wasn't any room,' she paused, 'I asked Greg to load it, but there was no room.'

'That sucks, Mom.'

'I know.'

Mom went to stroke his face, but he sat back in the seat and pulled Luke to his lap. The dog repositioned himself and compliantly continued to lick his paws.

'Why do we always have to move?'

'You'll be closer to Dad.'

'Yeah, but we liked it here.'

'You liked the last place too.'

'This is the city.'

'And there'll be lots of other kids.'

'But no place to play.'

'There's a field across…'

'I know.'

Greg put his head in at the window and said, '$15.66.'

'Well, maybe you can paint the basement walls if you like,' she said, handing Greg the money. 'What do you think, hon? He could paint the walls, couldn't he?'

Greg's knuckles rang on the car roof and Luke perked his ears. 'Sure, why not?' he said and withdrew.

When the boys got back from the bathroom Sam tried to get out, but Tom complained about sitting in the bad seat and Sam, at Mom's insistence, scooted over instead. Luke forsook the open window to settle back in his lap and everyone else got as comfortable as possible.

Mom searched the radio again and managed to find a local country station. The boys started a game of license-plate alphabet, and Travis got a slug bug on Tom. Tom fumed and threatened to hit him back. Greg drove and Mom refereed. Luke began to drift off beneath Sam's petting and Sam absorbed some of his warm calm.

A short way out of town they turned off the highway into a gravel U-shaped parking lot. Logs were sunk into the ground to mark each space and the small brown building behind them looked deserted. Greg braked and the boys looked up. The engine idled.

'Don't look at me,' Greg said, 'I'm not telling them.'

'We have to.'

'Yeah, but it's not right, and you should have done it earlier.'

'Fine,' Mom shot, and opened the door. She went to the trunk and came back with a small travel cooler. 'We're going to eat, boys.'

Meal times were always a point of great excitement in their house, even if it was just peanut butter sandwiches and single serving Kool-Aid grenades, and even if the house was a car. She passed the things to Greg and told him to get everything set. 'I'll take Luke to pee.'

Travis wanted to get out of the car too, but Greg kept him inside. Mom took Luke to a spot near the building and knelt. Sandwiches were passed around and there was almost a fight because Sam and Tom both wanted fruit punch when there was only one. Fortunately, Greg found a second hidden under Mom's diet cola.

'You guys have to promise to be good for your mom. No more fighting. No crying. Can you do that?' he said, holding Sam's fruit punch hostage.

Everyone was working the peanut butter around in their mouths when Mom came back. Closing the door, she whispered 'Okay,' and the car was put into drive.

Between a full mouth and the realization that Luke wasn't with them, Sam was speechless. His hand dropped to the broken handle.

There he was, a little dog with the heart of ten, tied to a post as they pulled away. He sat still, his miniature brawler's chest puffed and his eyes marble. There was no yipping or pulling against his leash, just the cool confidence of one friend at a crossroads waiting for another.

Sam forced himself to swallow the mashed lump of peanut butter and crystallized honey.

'Hey, you forgot Luke,' Travis said, and turning to Sam reiterated, 'they forgot him.'

'Come on. You knew,' Greg said placing a hand on their mom's thigh. 'We can't keep dogs at the new house.'

'It's Luke,' Tom said.

Feeling his trembling features harden as Luke slipped away behind the trailer Sam said simply, 'He's going to die.'

Mom's voice broke and struggled when she tried to tell them that the building, without windows or signs, was an animal shelter.

'Don't worry. He'll be fine. He is Lucky Luke after all, isn't he?' Greg said, and Mom nodded vigorously, as though to convince herself of the truth in his words. Sam didn't talk back or cry. Tears would have been useless, and instead he stared stoically ahead.

The highway stretched out before them, and they were following it to where the nickel sky began to tarnish. Somewhere in the numb silence Sam sensed his sleeve being tugged. He looked over and Travis thrust a folded piece of paper, a map, into his hands and said, 'You'll keep it safe, won't you?'

Ruth T Calway
A Progressive County

The lovely meadow, submissive in the sun,
lays down its rustling seed,
bleeds where the crushing wheels run.

I had walked at dawn a helpless walk.
The sorrel, the ragwort and the lace of yarrow
wore my sorrow like buds that would not break
for being already broken.
Twelve years we had lived side by side
through hope and the fleet of happiness,
through the wither of happiness
and hope rising again.

As I walked
the skin of the field crawled, all the glory
of the morning sinking. And then the stink
of the fumes and the metal
bearing down. The laughter of men
in shiny-hard, cartoon hats—what need had *they*?
In the palpable air of high summer
in the sweet hay a pulse wildly beating
in the petrified grass and leaves.
They had never been stalked like this.

I could not bear to watch but watch I did
for the bearing of witness, for the love
I bore the meadow, all it bore—
the birds of the ground
and the tall trees, the streak of fox
leaving its musk on the warm morning grasses,
the ponies, whisking the summer away,
the field mice outwitting the cats, and stoking
their cheeks with all the plump of harvest;
hedgehogs whistling and snuffling,

and rabbit, weasel, deer and stoats
all in the headlights of so many nights.

And now the raped
field and all its yield is gone forever,
the guts of the clay spilling inside out,
and all that is left
clings to the hedgerows,
nettle and thistle in pitiful defence,
clutches of fur and feather.

The sky has blanched white.
The ghosts of the last trees are lumbering
in their old skins, like giants
with nowhere to go.

Only
an old Scots pine stands now, defiant.
Life and death underneath it twitches.
One more night left of thirty-thousand.
One more night to imagine
in its branches, winged horses,
magic carpets, moonlit witches.

I stumble over the sorrel-red earth
drying to ragwort yellow, streaks of iron
raw and blue like veins,
my world turned inside out.
In the horrified evening I kneel,
open my saddle-bag of seed
so full of morning
and gather cones from under the pine.

On the skyline an insect-like
huge yellow form screeches
its victory and lifts
high its sword.

I scatter the seeds in another county.

Ruth T Calway
Not a Plot at All

Something had happened to the bonfire. All week it had sat there, humbly, resigned to whatever fate threw at it, until a couple of days ago when it started looking a bit too pleased with itself for Meg's liking. 'You're getting above yourself,' she had commented, 'sitting there like Manes[1] himself. How can I set you alight, looking like that?'

'Oh, you're more than a match for 'ee,' had quipped Peter the Birdman, who was the only peace-loving neighbour who ever came near Rookery Tops. 'All the same,' he added, scratching the white, pointy beard that always seemed to scratch him back, 'remember what old Blakey said.' And he shook his head, wisely.

'Yes,' said Meg. 'What?' she said. Blake had said so much.

'I don't remember,' said Peter. 'I were 'oping 'ee would.'

'Oh,' said Meg, and they had stood there companionably for a while, taking it in turns to smoke Peter's pipe.

Anyway, as I was telling you, it was a couple of days ago that the bonfire appeared to be perking up, and that was after Meg had lugged that red carpet down from the attic — the one that had been mouldering away in Blake's old sea-chest for years — and dragged it to the bonfire's feet. These were wooden feet, of course, made of pallets that had rotted in the middle; there were legs, too, of furniture long gone to the dogs. She had decided not to be sentimental about things any more. The sea-chest itself had a lucky escape, since she simply could not move it. Mind you, the carpet had been heavier than expected, as though, to keep track of time, it had absorbed into its weft and warp the weight of eight attical years.

The bonfire had also been fed logs too big for the wood-burner; lop and top; a whole Leyland Cypress. No doubt about it, thought Meg, it had been over-indulged. She had wondered if it might get ideas and lumber off into the sunset.

'Run out on me and you're finished,' she had warned it darkly, only yesterday. It had stared back at her woodenly, stuffing itself

---

[1] *In 3rd Century Persia, Manes set up a religious system based on the eternal conflict between light and dark.*

with leaves. Now, it had gone.

Through the kitchen window, the sun glanced back at her as it waved shadows across the garden, before slinking off behind the woodshed. A heap of half-digested leaves still covered the plot where the bonfire had been, covertly smoking. A breeze sprang up just then, and scuppered the leaf pile, trying hard to make it look natural. It all felt a bit, well, conspiratorial.

It was still afternoon, but an afternoon in November, as her erstwhile husband, Dan, would have said, does a spot of glorious death and knocks off early. So Meg lit the candles anyway, the smell of sulphur briefly overpowering the frankincense of Autumn and the spices of Meg's cooking. Yet, even headier than these, something else was in the air.

They were coming.

Dan came in from the front garden looking like a laughing cavalier, his musket smoking. It was unlike him to disturb the rooks at roosting time, but they had looked fair to freefall and wiffle well into the dusk. They had clamoured mightily, and long after curling back to their high birches, shuffled and vibrated like a fretful parliament. Ben joined Dan in the hallway.

'We've got something for you,' Dan said. 'Show her, Ben.' Dan nudged the boy. Both their faces and shirts were smudged with gunpowder. Ben opened his sooty hand.

'Musket balls, Auntie Meg! Found them in that old oak stump we've been firing at—they're the real thing. Four hundred years old.'

'Wow,' said Meg, 'still there! Amazing.' She peered at the silver shot. 'The past is always closer than we think.' She made an ironic face at Dan who winked at Ben who nodded happily. He and the boy, both dirty blonde, might have been father and son. And for maybe eight seconds there was a blissful sense of their little world being remarkable, and harmonious. Sadly, Meg's habitual radar where Dan and Ben's free existence was concerned soon hit a target and began to bleep. What oak stump?

'What oak stump?' she asked aloud. Dan chucked his bearded chin eastward.

'Oh, no, Dan, not Crusty's meadow! You've been shooting on Crusty's land?'

The rooks jeered. The sun blushed. Dan and Ben looked unrepentant. As far as they were concerned, it was Meg's land in spirit and therefore Crusty had no real claim on it.

'He didn't see us,' offered Ben.

'Oh, so you made it your aim to alert old misery-guts to your eternal presence, with the loudest muskets in the Company!' Meg's voice rose a decibel or two and she worried the silver shot in her palm with the thumb of her other hand. Ben looked askance. Dan looked chuffed.

'Ooh, thanks,' he said.

Some things, thought Meg, were best just left to run their course. She returned to musing quietly over the eight tiny musket balls. They were gnarled as dried seeds and as she rolled and scrunched them together, heat generated. 'Oh, uh, by the way, do tell me,' she added, softly, but with a seemingly casual overtone more sensitive souls might be wary of, 'where's my bonfire?' Dan and Ben stopped beaming and looked furtive.

'It was there yesterday,' offered Ben.

'So was history,' said Meg, looking up, 'and *it's* still here.'

There was a brief silence; Ben's eyebrows conceded something and he cocked his head while Dan looked up at the ceiling as though history might well go up in smoke at any time. He was trying hard to look affronted. Meg pressed her advantage. 'You shot it, didn't you?' She folded her arms and looked directly into those familiar blue eyes. 'You shot my bonfire.' She could hear, through the open door, that there were disconcertingly sniggerish tremors from the birch tree parliament.

'Ah,' said Dan. 'I was wondering when you'd miss it.' He ducked as Meg's fist made a feint for his chest and then, with unerring tactic, released the silver shot down the back of his draw-strung shirt.

'Straight through the heart,' choked Dan, dropping to his knees.

'Why do I do this, year after year,' Meg wondered, watching her visitors advancing like dusk moths, drawing closer and closer to the candlelit cottage. All dressed in Civil War costume, mostly King's Men and Camp Followers. Just ahead of them, twirling and mincing, was Greg, doing his camp—very camp—speech to the

Followers. She could almost see their laughter curling in the jaunty air. Though they were still beyond the garden gate, and the dogs were delirious, Meg could hear guffaws and glimpsed the formidable Kate, in full bosom, clipping Greg across the ear. Essential as they were to the army, there was no King's Shilling for the Baggage—that is, the cartloads of supplies and victuals in which category women and children were included. Nor for the so-called Camp Followers, who were mostly entertainers, and recorders of the battles. Kate might have got it, though, that Shilling—she would have used her particularly potent blend of seduction and intimidation and taken on the Paymaster General himself.

Greg tripped up to the garden gate, fathoming its bolt fussily. He eyed the musketeers with preposterous coyness, pouting his lips to the women from behind his shield as they clumped through. The dogs were grinning and weaving; Fable ran back to the house in high excitement to gleam her wolfhound eyes at Meg, returning to the visitors with a ball in her mouth which Fife quickly stole. Fable could never hang on to anything for long, for laughing. Meg laughed too, watching Greg. She knew well, and from many a quarter, that he was definitely all man from his beard to the bottom of his bucket-top boots, and this made his performance all the more hilarious. Sure enough, he reverted to type, swift as a rapier, when a skirmish broke out, with Oliver drawing his sword.

'Have a care, sir,' he warned Greg, 'I will unman you yet!' Hamming it up to the nines, he stepped back to make his point, right into the plot where the bonfire had been. Meg held her breath. Everyone froze. The three dogs, who had joined in the skirmish with relish, moved first, breaking rank to sniff among the brown paper ribbons of the astonished garden. Then Kate—dear Kate—put her hands on her hips, looking archly at the circle that had once held the proud bonfire.

'What treachery is this?' she cried, ' what . . . Gunpowder Plot?' and everyone laughed with relief except Oliver who, uncrossing his iron from Greg's, had stepped smartly out of the circle, making the old sign for warding off evil. Some of the company did likewise—Meg had not yet, after all, made her protective presence known—but at that moment Ben cannoned through the kitchen and Meg was distracted by a candle falling over. Greg saw the boy striding out, wrestled the leather football from Fife and kicked it to Ben, who fired it right into the full skirts of Cornelia Owen.

It was a good goal, thought Meg, since Cornelia wore far too many starchy petticoats and being 'descended from Boudicca herself,' as she frequently reminded everyone, might be enlivened by a brawl. With her hennaed hair and general magnificence at Marston Moor with her battle cry and all, thought Meg, perhaps she was right about Boudicca; but the woad was overdoing it a bit, all these centuries on. She put her hand to her mouth as she watched the small drama un-scuffling. No, she had to give old Corny her due, ancient fire in her blood or not, she took the knocks like a gentlewoman—though the ball was never seen again.

All faces now, white with dusk, alight with eagerness, were turned towards Meg's kitchen window. Meg's kitchen looked back through the leads, swaying a bit in the vapour of mulled wine and with the difficulty of appearing sober when all the lit tapers were squiffy and lolling and the racks of drying herbs and flowers were reviving with heady distillations of their own. Meg's mull was always very free with the brandy, well known for all kinds of restoration.

The candle flames, idly licking up the remaining light, guttered as a gust of wind bolted around the half door, now flung wide. But as Meg turned to receive her guests, the flames began to stream up, up to the top panes of the window, while those candles that were on the tables and shelves stretched themselves into lines of fire that exceeded the length of wax. Meg reached up too, welcoming her guests; the red in her nut-brown hair flickering and her eyes drinking in the minute changes time had drawn.

To its relief, and Meg's, the warmth of the intoxicated kitchen coaxed out the autumn elixir and sea salt absorbed by the gathering, like a cure. The room stopped spinning and concentrated for singular moments upon the taste and scent of other lives and abodes, the essences of which were captured in the wool of their clothes. Meg allowed herself to be surrounded. She stood still by the huge oak table in her spangled black dress, slender as a starling. So here they were. Here they were again, with faces and attitudes profoundly known and dear to her.

They have come, thought Meg, to warm themselves upon my

fire, and return some light into my dark rooms.

'Where's the bonfire?' mouthed Kate from the hallway where she was helping Ben stash all the irons, cloaks and spurs.

'Civil War,' Meg mouthed back, indicating herself and Dan and making a cutthroat gesture.

'Dan,' called Kate, to where he was serving mull from the hot range, and booming with bonhomie, 'you look like Guy Fawkes, darling.'

'I know how he felt.'

'There is always the fire inside,' laughed Meg.

It was a night when the moon kept going out. A few spirit lamps were lit; not rush-lights, there was too much smoke already. And what with the fire, and the candles, what with the shadow-dancing, and the darkly intoned folk songs offset by the gleam of tin whistles, and the odd clear soprano (no-one was quite sure where from), the ambience was very living history. Each face was provocatively illumed and shadowed by firelight drawing out the different ages that co-exist in every countenance. The Company were twelve in number; some looked so alike they were interchangeable. Their shadows re-enacted them, and they, their shadows.

In the living room, Ben was showing off the musket balls to the assembly, among whom Kate and Oliver flirted. Meg and her dogs were skilfully weaving around the bodies in the kitchen; she busy with the laying out of food, they, with the laying on of paws. 'By the blood of... what was that,' expostulated Robbie, as an invisible Fife put a paw on his knee from under the kitchen table and licked the bare skin exposed between kilt and stocking. Fife wagged his tail and began a long explanation. I think it was then, just as the old black cat with one blue eye was walloped from under the table by Fife's tail, that Ben stole past, into the night, but I can't be sure. The door latch did rattle, the hinges did squeak, and the uprising gale outside did get wind of it, and came skulking.

'Who needs a bonfire, anyway,' boomed Dan, pausing to tease out cinnamon sticks from the brew on the range, 'with mull like this? Go on!' he chuckled amid cheers, ladling more of the potent liquid into the tankard of Cornelia Owen. 'It'll warm the cockles of your heart!' And he winked at Meg.

At that moment, the door burst open with a howl, and a gust of wind did a few triumphant laps of each room before scampering up the stairs. Many of the candles snuffed it.

'Cracking night for a blaze, though,' enthused Robbie, when peace was restored. He was striking several matches at once, as though this might bring re-enforcement. Fife's ears drooped with match-cinder and he looked, hangdog, at Meg. She crooked him a look of sympathy and he wound back to her side of the table. As for the table, a few more bright sparks were nothing to what it had lived through.

'Do hearts have cockles, I wonder?' mused Cornelia, with a blue-woad blush. Patrick mercifully stopped beating the dirge he was always playing on that wretched bodhrun.

'Sure to God they do!' he protested. 'I've seen them, so I have.' And he went on to expound—with huge blarney and raunchiness —about his open-heartedness, and the cockles therein. The Company were round with laughter. Meg shook her head and flicked another cat from the table.

'Phoenixes,' stated Peter the Birdman, quietly, from the titbit corner. Stone me, he made me jump. I had forgotten he was there. He champed on his pipe and swivelled his head to look at Meg, now pecking about inside the range. She bumped her head as she rose to look at him, her face aflame.

'Phoenixes?'

'Phoenixes,' he repeated, stuffing the bowl of his pipe and tabbing the tobacco down with a tobacco thumb. 'They need bonfires.' And he brought out the lighter that was almost the size of a pistol and indulged for a minute in the fire-breathing for which he was famous. Clouds of cherry-flavoured smoke filled the kitchen. Meg was glad. It screened the acrid smoke curdling out from the range. She burnt the pumpkin pies every year. A familiar squawk of laughter came in with the owl-hoots on the wind.

*

There was, once upon a time, a story going around about Old Blakey being a Pirate, but this was, in fact, inaccurate. Blakey was a parrot. It is true that he belonged to a Pirate, but the Pirate's name was Billy, and it all got mixed up, the way things do over time.

Blakey could talk for England. Unfortunately, he did this in a Jamaican accent so it took a very good all round sort of ear—or a Jamaican, of course—to understand him. No-one really knew where he came from originally, or how old he was, though he was at least a hundred in Billy's time, which was a very long time indeed.

Left to Meg's care, Blakey lived for years in the old sea chest that had once contained everything that great-uncle Billy had owned. Meg had burned the wooden leg years ago.

That chest had been all around the world. When Billy died, Blakey refused to take to any perch. He just lived in the chest, sleeping in that rolled up Persian carpet, more like a human being than a bird. Now and again he'd have a day in the garden imitating everything the rooks said and did, which irritated them immensely, and he would crow about it for days on end.

Poor old Blakey. He died in that chest, on top of the Persian carpet that no-one was allowed to touch. Meg had once thought it beautiful, but now it just made her sad to see it.

So that is how an ancient roll of carpet had come to be at the foot of a bonfire, in Meg's garden, on November the fifth, in the last year of another century. Exactly *how* the bonfire was moved to make a run for it, no-one will ever know for sure. But it had something to do with—well, I might as well tell you.

That early afternoon, in the gold of the day, Meg was out in the lowland fields with the dogs, harvesting chestnuts to roast that evening. Having filled her basket, she walked the long way home, up across the cliffs. Here, she was out of sight of Crusty's meadow, which sloped down to the east of Rookery Tops. What with the waves crashing below her, she was also out of knowing earshot of musket fire.

Dan and Ben were in the garden, shooting the Leyland Cypress. The whole bonfire had begun to smoulder.

'Here, Ben, grab an end of this carpet.'

'Why for?'

'Stifle the sparks.' They heaved and hoed and dragged damp leaves along with the huge roll of carpet onto the bonfire. They sat down on top to wait for the smoke to die down.

'Here, Ben.' Dan had one of those looks on.

'What now?'

'I've got an idea.'

'Is it anything like the last idea?'

'Not in the sense of blowing anyone up, no . . . '

'Oh. Good.'

'...though, you've got to admit, if it had worked . . .'

'Uncle Dan... '

'Sorry, son.'

'No edge of the cliff stuff, either?' Ben asked anxiously, as Dan nodded him towards the other end of the carpet which he was now dragging away.

'Not this time, my boy. Keep your powder dry.'

'Uncle Dan, where are we taking this?' Ben was breathless. 'It's darned heavy.'

'Tell you what, we'll drag it out,' said Dan, putting his end down under the birch trees and indicating Ben should do the same. They stooped and laboured over the carpet's long-creased folds and rolls, unaffected by scorches. Up in the yellow breeze, the rooks began clawing at the air and stave-fulls of jet black quavers tumbled out into it, one on top of another.

'What's up with them?' asked Ben. With a toss of his beard, Dan indicated the muskets strung across their backs.

'But they know we never hit anything.' Ben rolled his eyes heavenward.

'Blow me down, did you hear that?' asked Dan, pausing for a second and looking up into the birches. 'Sounded more like a parrot than a rook.'

'Now I'm really spooked,' said Ben. They began to unfold the last humps of silken carpet. The rooks were screaming.

'They've lost the plot,' said Dan.

*

'Where's Ben?' asked Meg, as the revelry rose to its height and there was still no sign. Dan had also disappeared. 'If they're not back by midnight…'

'We'll all turn into pumpkins!' chorused the gathering. Meg sighed. They were almost out of control, now; worse, Robbie had brought out his bagpipes. Fleet, the setter, who until now had been on point in the hall waiting for them to make their charge from under the cloaks they had been buried beneath, pipes protruding like horns, buried her long ears under her paws.

'Come on,' yelled Kate, rosy as a pomegranate. 'Let's take the logs from the woodshed and make another bonfire, away from Meg's plot—somewhere else.' She battled with the door and the door battled back, out into the wind that almost bowled her down. But Kate was a woman not easily overturned. 'Come on, troops!' And with the entire recruitment of the raggle-taggle carousers, she charged out into the night, brandishing her bosoms, to raid the woodshed. Soon, right in front of Rookery Tops, a whole regiment of King's Men, grinning like pumpkins, were toasting Cornelia Owen with their leather tankards, as she stood abreast a huge pile of logs and sticks and attempted to light it with a candle and one of her petticoats.

'Oh dear,' said the deserted Meg to Peter, sharing with him a twist of a smile, 'she can billow on those logs until she's blue in the face… but I'm the only one who can light the bonfire.'

'And it's gone,' stated Peter, taking his pipe from his mouth and nodding at it wisely.

'Mmm,' demurred Meg.

'And Dan and Ben. Gone.'

'Mmm.'

'You remember what…?'

'Yes, said Meg. 'He said…' and she bent over to whisper in Peter's ear, taking care not to snag herself on his beard. The Birdman's apple cheeks grew rounder and shinier and his sky-blue eyes wept, which was what he did in lieu of laughing.

'Is that so? Is it so?' he chuckled, 'ee were a salty old bird, and no mistake.' And he exploded into a merry fit of coughing and flapping of arms during which Meg was moved to relight his pipe for him, and breathe in the scent of ripe cherries.

*

What the rooks knew was what Blakey knew. What Blakey knew was what Billy knew and what Billy knew was that the carpet was studded with eight heavy gold sovereigns. With which, Dan, and Ben—our ecstatic explorers of the legendary qualities of old carpet—had bought Crusty's meadow, that very afternoon. For Meg. In her memory.

So there they all were, restored to excellent spirits with the effect of Meg's centuries-old brandy, singing away before the sails of petticoat, for all the world re-enacting the triumph of a witch who would not burn. Every year they liked to think that she was still here, talking to them, moving amongst them. Some were closer to her than others. Some were more present than others.

A single musket shot sundered the night. The wind died. Rooks froze in their chariot branches. All faces turned to the hill where the meadow sloped eastward. There was a flicker of light, then another and another, as a breeze returned to fan a bonfire high and wild. A great cheer resounded from the rank and file below. Dan and Ben were silhouetted on the gunmetal skyline, arms aloft and ashes quavering all around them.

It was a magnificent bonfire, comprising an entire hedge-full of cypress that had lost the will to live—the hedge that had once formed the border between Meg's land and Crusty's meadow. It brought light into Meg's dark rooms. She came in through the front garden of Rookery Tops, her musket smoking. It felt good. She hadn't fired a shot in that meadow for four hundred years.

But what about the original bonfire—the one that something had happened to? Let me show you something, down on the eastern slope of the meadow, below the birches. An enclosure made of rotting pallets and old furniture, interwoven with lop and top, out-sized logs and one whole but completely shot Leyland Cypress. Inside this little plot, a beautiful old Persian carpet stretched out in a spell of smoky moonlight, just waiting. I don't know what for, but it was something to do with what old Blakey said.

Gavin Goodwin
Poems in Verse and Prose

Swimming in Nice

In high afternoon sun
we slip down wet pebbles
that waves drag from under us,
teetering into shallows of a turquoise sea.

I dive in first,
warm sleepy skin startled awake.
You plunge in after me.

Treading water, we look out.
Sea merges into sky
with no exact horizon.

We know that soon
we'll be living miles apart,
and postcards on bookshelves
will invite us to remember

how here, buoyant in the water,
sun on our faces,
we draw close, share a kiss.

St Francis of Assisi Cathedral, Nice

She drops coins into a slotted box,
picks up two red candles
and lights them before Mary.

To her right stands St Francis
with skin brown as his robes,
his arms and his gaze held upwards.

I watch in silence
as she walks to the aisle chair of the middle row
and sits at the centre of the church.

She bows her head before
an elevated, crucified Christ,
his agony almost a silhouette
against low light.

I think of *her* suffering,
a suffering she never lets congeal to bitterness.
Though no longer the Catholic she was raised,
there in prayer, she emanates a silent faith.

Driving to the Reservoir

We sit in the back seat,
separated by the boat sail
that rests on my shoulder
in a canvas sheath.
I hold it steady with my hand
and gaze out of the window.
You purse your lips on my finger.

Fields of hops are stretching
across the flat lands of Kent.
Your kiss sparkles through me.

The Empty Flat

The green curtains taken down,
the desk dismantled. The T.V. sits
powerless in my parents' attic. Stacks of books
collapsed into bags, and removed —
all trace of us vacuumed away

except the dust on the window
that the light passes through,
the way it did those mornings we knew
weren't to last. I made hot chocolate
and toast, you lay sleeping.

That light still shining through.
You waking up miles away.

The Return

My broken suitcase
in the hallway   the kettle
bubbles to the boil

through the moonlit garden
cat pads toward the kitchen

she hands me a cup
finely printed
with lily of the valley

in bed her cheek on my shoulder
cat slinks back into moonlight

sun through white netting
I take a book from her shelf
she snores softly

dish of kibble for the cat
kettle bubbles to the boil

I hand her a cup
finely printed
with lily of the valley

Alone Together

She stands in lamplight at the bedside,
pyjama bottoms tied with red cotton cord.
Lately I have only heard her voice
crackling off a satellite, through a fog
of white noise, phone pressed against my ear.

On this moonless night she is close,
her voice clear. 'You will never really know
how I feel,' she says sadly. 'Even in love
we're alone.' After a day's travel,
moving into lamplight, I touch her hand.

Remembering Siena

Resting your elbows on the kitchen table,
shoulders like caramel from the sun,
the blue and white straps of your vest beam
off them and your hair is a mess of red curls.

For a moment unburdened, lost in a game
of cards, your laughter floats on warm air.
All pain has vanished from your eyes.

Outside: moonlight, the sound of cicadas.
Silhouettes of cypress trees taper to the sky.

Picking Bricks

Drinking tea in the bar before the film,
it's been a while, and our chat is awkward.
She says this process is like picking bricks
from an invisible wall between us.

I give her a present, nothing much,
a DVD of a show she likes.
After the film, we get back to my house
and realise we've left it behind in the bar.

The next day, in the park, late afternoon,
we pause under a beech tree. We smile
at each other: the wall has come down.
Invisible bricks scattered behind us,
we reclaim the present from the lost and found.

Match Day

The train is packed with blue shirts and sun burnt arms with green ink tattoos. The sun-baked steel of the door handle is almost too hot to open. An Indian porter on the platform inspires the chant: 'there ain't no black in the Union Jack.' A Japanese boy in a green cap squeezes himself between the toilet cubicle and the carriage door, his face to the window, gaze held on the hard, steel track. The men in blue shirts begin bouncing, the pungent sweat that polyester draws from armpits wafts among the smell of lager and cider. The train rocks on the rail. With a metallic squeal it stops, doors are thrown open, and blue pours from the carriage, spreads across the platform.

green cap removed
rim soaked in sweat—as the train moves
a faint breeze

Peacefully

I greet him warmly as if nothing is wrong. Attentive, I sit cross-legged in front of him, rubbing his soft beige belly, smoothing the black-flecked fur of his shoulder. I fetch a toy from his basket, one he hasn't played with for months. He snaps at it and chews enthusiastically. To look at him now you'd think he was fine, sitting on the quilt, a stuffed toy dangling from his lips. My mother stands by the window:

warm August morning
waiting for the vet
eyes pink with tears

The Mountain

From the car-park that our houses back on to, the four of us mount our bikes and ride on to the main road. Past the terrace houses that all look the same we pedal toward the mountain. We all wear tracksuit bottoms, t-shirts, baseball caps and trainers with logos—Nike, Adidas, Puma—stitched or printed prominently on them. The lack of this kind of sportswear would mean ridicule from the estate. Our mums work as cleaners at the hospital or on tills at the supermarket. Frightened their boys will be bullied, they are themselves bullied into spending half their wages to purchase these clothes with the coveted logos.

Turning off the road we enter lanes lined with hedgerows. Fields populated with black and white cows spread from each side of us. We ride over the Old Bridge where the rope swing dangles above a brown lagoon. The gradient grows steeper as the lane ends; we have to steer our way through the woodland, clenching the handle bars. We push our bikes over the exposed roots of pine trees, too dangerous to ride on, and finally carry them, hoisted on our shoulders, up to the peak. On top of the mountain we exhale deeply and let our bikes fall on to the rough grass. Before us the valleys descend in expanses of green fields, woods, and a curling silver stream; a red kite spreads the fan of his tail against the skyline. We turn to the estate behind us: although only a few miles away, its networks of concrete look small and unthreatening. We try to spot our houses. We trace the road that leads from the estate into town, under the motorway flyover and on to the horizon where our eyes strain to make out the grey blur of the Severn estuary. We stand there, our tracksuit trousers sticking to our thighs, taking gulps of the squash we've brought with us between deep draughts of air. It is a cool, clear day.

I don't know if any of us will ever live anywhere other than that estate we've just pedalled intensely away from. But today, as the wind hardens the sweat on our faces, we can see beyond it.

Robert D Leis
Daisy and the Black Squirrel

In the summer of 1983 Dad decided to add a wooden deck to the back of the house. It was a new house, finished only the year before. He promised Mom he'd let the sawdust settle before undertaking any new projects, but no sooner were the brooms put away than he was pacing out distances and hammering in stakes. Mom argued with him at first. She was a little woman compared to his burly physique, but all the more impressive for her ability to hold her own with a man who to me was the strongest man alive. If he needed Mom's permission, just as I did, than she was not as weak as her frame suggested. As far as I knew she was the only person who ever poked my father in the chest.

He'd start the day with a cup of coffee in one hand, a cigarette in the other, and a calculating look at the open space his deck would occupy. Before noon he'd be well into his work for the day, shirt discarded and sweating. He looked like a bear, chest and shoulders swollen with muscles, dark hair covering his entire body except for the pink scars that crisscrossed his forearms. They were welder's marks, he'd told me, and despite having no idea what kind of monster welders were, I was impressed.

Mom did her best to keep me out of my Dad's way while he worked, but I was a constant distraction anyway, sneaking into his workshop and poking through his toolbox until being ushered back inside and tied to Mom's apron. His other companion that summer was our black and grey German shepherd, Daisy. She was a lean, hard-muscled dog, with a shoulder scar courtesy of the winter coyotes that came out of the wooded hills when food became scarce. To the family she was a good dog, loyal and protective. To small animals she was a killer.

Most of her day was spent sleeping in the shadow of a big oak tree, stirring occasionally when a bird would land too close or a squirrel would risk its life for an acorn near her. Most of them knew better, they'd learned to leave our yard alone, which is probably why one of them was so determined to claim such plentiful, unoccupied real estate as its own. It was a black squirrel, from tip to tail. My Dad said he'd never seen one like it and that the other squirrels would never accept it.

'Why is that?' Mom asked him.

Dad used his shirt to wipe sweat off his face and chest. 'Squirrels are racist, of course.' She looked at him in doubtful amusement. 'But we're not,' he went on. 'We let any squirrel, of any color, forage here. Isn't that right?' The last remark was addressed to where I sat on a pile of planks. I nodded back, eager to take his side.

Mom snatched the shirt away from Dad and gave him an old towel she'd brought out for him, frowning at the dark stains on his white shirt. 'Let's hope Daisy agrees with you.'

Daisy didn't agree. Dad was hammering in corner posts when Daisy and the black squirrel were first introduced. She lunged after it, lips pulled back in a hungry snarl, the chain snaking through the grass behind her. The black squirrel ran straight across the lawn toward the hills and Daisy followed furiously until the chain snapped tight and she was jerked off her feet. Her snarls became coughs and after lingering to watch the squirrel retreat she sulked back to her tree.

'Well, you won't do that again,' Dad said to her.

He was wrong. Over the next several weeks the black squirrel came down often to gather acorns in the yard. Daisy would charge every time she saw it, getting yanked back by the thick chain. My Mom screamed in horror the first time she saw, afraid for the squirrel, and then for Daisy. She ran out into the yard and hugged the German shepherd, checking her over. When Daisy rolled onto her back and started wagging her tail Mom gave her a sharp slap and told her not to chase the squirrel. I'd already learned that dogs couldn't understand complicated things like that, but I'd also learned not to presume I knew more than Mom.

By the first week of August my Dad had finished the foundation for the deck and was ready to add the base boards and railings. He was smoking a cigarette when he saw the black squirrel run across the grass right in front of Daisy. It was a game that had gone on for weeks, but this time the squirrel stopped, turned around, and watched as almost a hundred pounds of fur, teeth, and anger came charging. Ten feet away Daisy's muscles tightened for the kill. At three feet the squirrel still hadn't moved. My Dad yelled at Daisy to stop but the pumping in her brain was too loud for her to hear. Then the chain went tight just in front of the black squirrel. Daisy, who had put all her power into the kill, let out a horrible choking yelp. A lesser dog would have broken its neck.

Dad called out to us, laughing, and we came out and saw Daisy barking and snarling, up on her hind legs, lunging over and over against her chain at something just beyond her reach. The black squirrel was also upright, just two feet in front of Daisy and watching her in what could only be described as amusement.

'It's got her range,' Dad said to my Mom. He smiled at me through his beard and pointed to where Daisy pulled against her chain.

'Her what?' My Mom asked.

'Her range,' he said. 'Instead of running for the trees it stopped when Daisy's chain ran out.'

Mom looked at the scene in disbelief. 'Squirrels aren't that smart.'

Dad raised his eyebrows to her and gestured toward the squirrel. It was gathering fallen acorns with a deliberate lack of speed, just out of Daisy's reach. Daisy looked like she would choke herself to death trying to get at it. Mom implored Dad to make her stop. He called to her and she reluctantly came to his side, glaring at the squirrel over her shoulder.

'Can't you chain her up in front?' Mom asked.

He shrugged in response. 'She keeps me company.'

All that week the squirrel came down and gathered acorns in our yard. Always close enough to annoy Daisy but never within her range. Dad said it would taunt Daisy endlessly, running just out of reach and then turning to watch her choke herself. Laughing, he would tease Daisy when she returned ashamed to his side.

'Black squirrel six, Daisy zero,' he would say.

By late August Dad had finished the deck. It was huge, stretching across the entire back of the house. The wood was painted and sealed and needed only time to dry before Mom could fill the flower-pots that he'd built into the corners. I helped him clean up and put his tools away. When we finished he sent me inside to get him a beer and then we sat together in the grass under Daisy's tree. Her tail started wagging when we joined her. I rubbed her stomach and Dad scratched at his beard before opening the beer and offering me the first drink. I tasted it and he chuckled while I struggled to keep a sour look off my face.

He saw the black squirrel coming toward us and pointed it out to me, at the same time grabbing Daisy's collar. He told me to get away from the chain and I moved to his other side. Daisy growled and showed her teeth but knew better than to pull away from her master's grip. Dad couldn't help but laugh while the black squirrel ran back and forth across the lawn, trying to taunt Daisy into motion. We sat there for a long while and Daisy finally settled down and just watched the squirrel. My Dad released his grip but commanded her to stay. She whined and looked at him. He stroked her fur affectionately but repeated the command for her to stay still.

The next day Dad got up and took his coffee outside as usual. He hooked Daisy up to her chain and sat against the tree, lighting a cigarette and looking out over our yard toward the hills. That day there were one or two finishing touches on the deck for him to take care of, and he even spent a couple hours pulling weeds out of the garden, but he kept glancing to the hills and took more than his usual number of breaks under the tree with Daisy. Mom brought his lunch when it was time, and his book too when he asked. Accustomed to his ways she said nothing when he spent the afternoon reading in the sun. Even as the light started to fade he found something to do, near the deck, and Mom thought it was cute how proud he was of it, assuming he was reluctant to finish the job.

As afternoon settled into evening the black squirrel came down its tree and strutted toward the lawn. Daisy didn't see it until it sprinted across the grass right in front of her nose. She lunged for it, missed, and then gave chase. The black squirrel ran twenty feet out and then turned. Dad stopped working and looked up.

The squirrel, so confident in its own cleverness, didn't move as Daisy came after it. It never suspected that my Dad would meddle in the territorial issues of the animal kingdom. That he would be tired of watching his old friend taunted. That before hooking her to the tree that morning he would give her another ten feet of chain.

Robert D Leis
Icarus in Flight

A warning echoed in the air behind him but he was too far ahead, soaring toward the city. He grinned, looking down at the ploughed fields and the neat lines that ran over the hills, framing circles around the few remaining trees. Birds glared down at him from above and he rose to meet them. They veered, flapping hard to get away from their unnatural cousin. Icarus flexed his shoulders and spun through a low cloud, cool moisture bathing his skin before he emerged above a ship making its way to port. It was set low in the water, heavy with goods from the mainland, and he saw men scurrying like insects through the rigging to trim back the sails. A large figure stood on the foredeck, guiding the vessel through the reefs with the confidence of a local man.

Warm wetness touched Icarus's arm and dried instantly. Even at this height he tasted salt in the air. He let the current take him higher to where the air was lighter and faltered for a moment, pulling in deep unsatisfying breaths. Small specks appeared in his vision. He wiped at them and saw he had moved higher, the birds some distance below.

He felt blood running down his forearm and looked to see wax mixed with sweat dripping from his elbow, vanishing toward the clouds. As if waiting for him to notice, the wings started to dissolve. First one, then several small feathers disentangled themselves and spun away. He struggled to retain lightness, willing flesh and muscle to hold the air beneath him. He grunted and tried to lower himself, twisting his arms to allow the current over the wings, but instead of gradually descending he did an aerial stumble that whipped him around. Each white feather chose a new direction and soon all that was left of his wings was the wax dripping down his back and arms. Gravity reclaimed its power over Icarus and he plummeted straight down, betrayed by the skies which had welcomed him.

Fear gripped him low in the belly but he never looked down at the water rushing to meet him. He clawed frantically toward the sky as the birds he had looked down upon became smaller, the taste of salt became stronger, and the heavens slipped away.

Robert D Leis
Three Poems

Sweeping

When shadows crept in from under the door
I jumped to my feet and dashed into the kitchen,
stamping my foot until Mom gave me the broom.

I ran up and down the stairs, in and out of rooms,
sweeping them back into their dark homes,
under beds, corners, and behind closet doors.

Basement

Cold concrete walls and spider webs
contrast the cardboard castle behind the weight bench.

We train in the basement,
Dad and me.

He pounds his fists into a sandbag,
I slay dragons with a plastic sword.

He and She

She isn't really mad at him. She takes a swing but fights hard not to smile. He's not fighting, he's grinning like a fool, backpedaling, hands thrown up in defense. She's a half foot shorter than he is but growing with every menacing step she takes. He apologizes, enough to slow her charge, but too little to be forgiven.

She stands, hands on hips and a grin finally making its way to her face. Happy he still has her attention, he promises to be good, and asks how he can make it up to her. She's just happy it's important to him.

This is how you flirt at thirteen. He does anything to elicit a response, and she does anything to keep him around on the way home, even feigning offense when none was taken.

Robert D Leis
from *Seran Vale*, a novel

With the war at the Wall raging to the east, Keida of the Panther tribe has sent men to kill Malaura and her son Mooki of the Lion. Dagnar, chief of the Lion and Malaura's husband, was killed at the wall, and Keida hopes to kill his wife and son, thus rendering the Lion leaderless and allowing him to sweep in and take their lands. Laiddos, an enemy of the tribes and citizen of Seran Vale, has followed these soldiers. He's curious to know if the tribes will remain united and thinks his answers lie with these Panthers who travel through Lion territory. His mission is to gather information and not to get involved in tribal affairs. If discovered he would be hunted mercilessly by members of either tribe.

Malaura wiped her hands down the front of her vest smearing chicken fat on the leather. She tossed the remains of the bird to Bors and heard a loud snap as the hound's jaws cracked down. Squirrels chased each other, hopping and coming down over the broken leaves. When she was a child her grandmother had told her they were the footsteps of pixies waiting to steal children and she had marched out into the woods with an iron spoon to challenge them.

She smiled at the memory and looked up at the goat path that led into the bowl of the valley, wider now since her son Mooki had taken the stock through to graze. Almost a man, Mooki had been angry he could not go with the warriors to the Wall. Instead he had been told to stay and care for the goats. Mooki knew better than to argue with his father, but as soon as Dagnar marched he had taken to temper. For days he railed to Malaura about his prowess as a fighter.

'He may need me,' he told her on the day his father left.

'Why will he need you, boy? You are not yet fifteen summers.'

'I can fight…'

'Of course you can fight,' she interrupted. 'You are Lion. But your father has spoken and tomorrow you take the goats. Now, go away.'

He had left for the high passes three weeks ago for the rutting season and would be back soon. The snows were less than a month off and Malaura hoped to see at least half of her females pregnant. This would allow her enough meat to see them through the following winter and the rest they could trade for grain. She would keep some of the skins for Mooki who outgrew clothes faster than she could make them.

Mooki had light-colored hair pulled back in the Lion's knot and the sharp angles of his face gave him the look of eagles. The muscles in his lean frame were just beginning to fill out and his shoulders stood wide and straight. He looked the way Dagnar did fifteen years before when he had asked Malaura to walk the Sacred Tree.

She was just a girl then but knew enough to turn him away. His eyes had been so serious and he had simply nodded and walked away. That summer he and other members of the Lion raided an eastern outpost. They were caught on the way there by rangers of the Seran Vale. Most of them were killed. Dagnar was brought back by two others and almost died of his wounds. She went to see him during his recovery and found herself admiring the deep scar he had gained across his chest.

'I failed,' he said when he awoke and saw her standing there.

'Yes,' she said. 'And I will not marry a boy.'

He bowed his head in acknowledgement then continued to stare at her. She walked back to the front of the tent and opened it. 'Become a man before another approaches me.'

He was fully recovered by later that fall when there was an attack on their village by warriors of the Panther. Lions lost their lives that day but Dagnar had claimed his first kill. He arrived at her tent with a fresh scar down his forearm and blood on his clothes. The next day they walked the tree in front of the elders and she became wife to the future Chief of the Lions.

Pulling off her gloves and running her fingers through her dark hair she looked east to where her husband led an army against the Wall. Thick pines covered the eastern side of the valley and the world lay quiet while she imagined listening to the distant battle. May Elyeigha guide him home to teach his son the way of the Lion, she thought.

Her eyes, once again, moved to the empty goat path.

*

Laiddos sat in the elbow of a large oak tree, his brown wool cloak and dark leather clothing making him nearly invisible. Chill night air moved across the valley in a low fog and a playful breeze crept through the branches and licked him softly. A fox crept out of its den and walked directly beneath the hidden ranger. It stopped suddenly and its ears flattened. It sniffed the air and tensed.

'Good evening,' Laiddos whispered from above it.

The startled fox turned quickly and made a dash for the den opening, changed its mind, and shot off into the darkness.

He had been trailing the tribesmen for six days deep into Lion territory. They stopped several hours before sunset and began to make camp. Assuming they were close to whatever they were looking for, Laiddos waited for them to settle in and then scouted ahead to see what it was that they were close to. He was surprised to find a single hut a few miles away from Sandstone; the largest Lion village in the southern territory. He pulled the hood of his wool cloak tight around his face to ward off the cold and stared at the small wooden house across the clearing. Smoke curled out of the stone and mortar chimney, drifting lazily up before the breeze scattered it. For nearly an hour he perched until he caught sight of its occupant.

She stood outlined in the doorway by the glowing fire behind her. Her bare arms were lean but well muscled. Her hair was pulled back tight, shaved on the sides in the way of the Lion. A huge boar-hound stood at her side gazing into the woods where Laiddos hid. It growled but didn't leave the woman's side. Her eyes were locked to the path, no doubt expecting the arrival of the warriors.

'Not yet,' she said to the hound.

Since when did the Lion tribe and Panther tribe share meat, Laiddos thought. Few of the easterners knew very much about tribal politics, but foremost amongst those were the Rangers who spent most of their lives guarding the borders; and even they knew very little. One thing Laiddos was sure of was that the Panther and Lion spent more time sticking knives in each other than talking. He wondered why the warriors were coming here. They were soldiers, not farmers, and there was nothing here that required warriors.

He watched her close the door and the portal of light winked out. After softly dropping to the earth, making no more noise than the wind, he then made his way through the darkness and back to the tribesmen's camp.

The axe split through and two pieces fell to the ground. Malaura set up another length of wood and in one swift smooth motion the blade came down and two more fell. Sweat rolled down her neck and chest but her breath came in relaxed equal measures. She would stack the wood against the walls of her house to protect against the wind and provide insulation during the frozen months. A fire needed to burn constantly during the worst of the season and running short of wood was a sure way of not being around in the spring.

Bors let out a deep growl. She looked up to see men emerging from the goat path, a dozen of them, all armed. Their battered armor showed signs of recent fighting, warriors returning from the wall. Their shaved heads and scarred faces identified them to Malaura as Panther warriors, far away from their lands and people.

She reached down and placed a calming hand on Bors but kept the other tightly curled around the handle of the ax. The center warrior was tall and well built. He wore a tight pelt vest over a grey wool shirt. A war axe was strapped across his back and she could see a long blade belted at his hip. His face was scarred in the fashion of the Panther. She had seen the marks before but had never seen such a significant number. Intricate shapes and symbols curled and negotiated their way over his entire face, around his ears, and down his neck to his chest where they disappeared under the vest. He had cruel eyes and for the first time she was glad Mooki was still in the high pastures. He spoke to a tribesman on his right and the warrior ran off toward her house. The rest formed a circle around her and the Leader came forward.

'You are Chief Dagnar's wife?' His voice was smooth and deep.

'I am.'

'You have a boy. Where is he?'

'He is with his Father at The Wall.'

The man's eyes grew cold. She stared him straight in the face and said nothing. Bors was still under her hand but his growl poured out like a thunderstorm and all of his teeth were on display. Malaura looked around to see the other men watching her, eyes expressionless. In the woods she thought she saw a movement but turned back as the tribesman who had walked into her house returned.

'There is no one else here,' he said to the leader.

She looked towards the goat path and this time she was relieved to see it empty. The leader nodded to the warrior, whispered something, and then the man ran back up the path.

'We stay here. Scout the area for signs of the boy,' he announced to the other warriors. 'If he's gone, he'll be back soon.'

'We should kill her and go,' said a short but powerfully built warrior.

'She will die after the…'

Before he finished Malaura released Bors and the hound, eager to be let off restraint, bunched his shoulders and lunged at the leader. Malaura was already turning with a double grip on the ax, swinging hard at a warrior on her left. The man was fast but he took a glancing blow that sent him staggering backwards. She pulled it back for another strike but was hit hard from behind and dropped to the earth. She heard Bors snarling but it sounded faint and distant. Suddenly the hound cried out and she tried to pull herself up. A boot slammed hard down on her back and she was pushed flat. She managed to turn her head to the side and looked up to see the leader pulling his knife out of Bors' side. The hound was still breathing but lying limp at the man's feet. She heard rather than felt something strike her a second time and then darkness.

Alaleh Mohajerani
from *Niku*, a novel

Little Tree

Mahin Banu Sameni came from a long line of Tehrani bazaar merchants. With hair like a soft, swift death and eyes that just knew better, the Sameni women married well above their social ranking. At the age of fifteen, Mahin Banu, the most luminous of her sisters by far, married Asqar Aqa Moftakhar, a slightly chubby young gentleman with maternal ties to the Qajar dynasty. By age nineteen, Mahin Banu had already given birth to three daughters. The eldest, named Mansureh but called Homa, died while still in her cot. The second, legally named Homa after the deceased first child but called Shuku, frequently became the unfortunate victim of Mahin Banu's unpredictable temper tantrums. The third was given an outdated religious appellation by the civil registry clerk, a name too hideous to mention, but was simply known in the family as Niku.

The Moftakhar House on Moftakhar Street

The Moftakhar house curled itself around Moftakhar Street in a fat droplet of paisley. When they first assigned surnames in Tehran, Asqar Aqa's father, Ali Aqa, chose the name Moftakhar because he had studied Arabic, and in Arabic *moftakhar* meant proud. In Persian, it translated loosely into gratis donkey. Alas, Ali Aqa's love of foreign languages blinded him to even the most conspicuous of Persian puns, and in the end Moftakhar it was.

Like their name, the Moftakhar family's home reflected an inherent, effortless sort of pride. No ostentatious gardens stood mocking passers-by in the front. No curlicued gates boasted of privileged luxuries within. Tall, pale brick walls wound around the entire back and side of the residence, as the Moftakhars were a private people who preferred to reserve the beauty of their gardens, and their women, for themselves. On the other hand, the gratis donkey in them frequently left the front door wide open to strangers, traded oil with amputated Arab merchants and allowed themselves to be robbed by the household staff of every last gold coin that sparkled in crystal vases in the salon.

The front of the Moftakhar house faced a dewy avenue called Jaleh, which ran adjacent to Moftakhar Street. Further down, Jaleh Avenue was filled with all sorts of shops. Ali-Labaniati's dairy shop, Hajji-Eye-Crust's grocery store, Hassan-Kebabi's kebab house, Chesty-Molesty's bakery. At this end, however, Jaleh Avenue was largely residential, though one could hardly call it quiet. Several other old Tehrani families built their houses here, rearing their minimum of half a dozen children each.

The main door of the Moftakhar house opened into a silk-carpeted corridor that stopped unsuspecting guests before they had a chance to remove their right shoe. It was like walking into the inside of a diamond—everything sunlit, iridescent and cut into delicate facets. The birds on the cream carpets appeared to fly off into the sky behind the glass at the end of the corridor. Crystal chandeliers and inlaid mother-of-pearl mirrors mingled as if at a fancy party. The sound of the fountain flirting with the pigeons in the garden and the smell of lunch being dressed downstairs like a fine lady, all met here in the corridor. It was such a contrast to the plain bricks of the outside of the house, such a sudden overwhelming of the senses, that only the occasional foul-mouthed child screaming through the courtyard could have broken the spell.

To the right of the glittering corridor was the large salon, where guests were received. To the left, the French dining room and French sitting room, which were in fact Persian, despite the sumptuous Louis XIV dining set, damask canapés, and sexy, curvy-legged tables. Everything else was decorated with the same motif—crystal chandeliers reigning over the rooms like sun gods; massive mother-of-pearl adorned chests, draped with dainty, gold-embroidered *termehs*[2]; crystal dishes and vases pouring out of the inlaid cabinets, filled to the brim with antique coins. And everywhere, silk carpets surging; wall to wall, room to room.

Downstairs, the basement was laid out in a similar, though slightly more somber manner. A long corridor ran directly parallel to the one above, with the kitchen and water storage to the left

---

[2] *termeh: traditional Persian embroidered cloth*

and the summer sitting and dining rooms to the right. Everything downstairs was duskier, heavier; all the furniture in cooler, moonlit colors. Blues and greys replaced the creams and beiges of the upholstery upstairs. Horses and deer substituted the birds and flowers of the carpets. In lieu of colossal chandeliers twinkled small starry lamps and silver candelabras with dangling crystal earrings.

But beauty kicked off its shoes and reposed once it reached the stony basement kitchen. With three fireplaces spitting flames like the *Azi Dahaka*[3], the kitchen was not lavishly decorated but was warm and happy, even during the bleakest of winters. It was where Ameh Shokat did all the family's cooking year-round and was generally acknowledged as her domain.

Behind the kitchen, at the end of the long basement corridor, was an even longer *hammam*[4], which absolutely nobody used. As the women of the family preferred to pack their wedding *termehs* with soaps and fruit, making a picnic out of the occasion, and as the men insisted on being lathered up and tossed about by burly professionals, the Moftakhars depended on public *hammams* for all their bathing necessities.

These rooms formed what was the main building of the Moftakhar home. Overlooking a large courtyard with a mosaic fountain in the middle, the brick structure was stuck between two weeping willows that constantly nagged at its windows and shed false, furry tears into the water below.

The rest of the courtyard was surrounded by eleven bedrooms, with the family rooms on one end, the servants' quarters on the other and the guestrooms looking out over the main building in-between. When the weather got hot, wooden summer beds were taken outside for the family and guests, with everyone tucked under the same kilim of stars.

East of the courtyard was another smaller, enclosed garden, which included an additional kitchen, used mainly to store coal, foodstuffs, and pickled goods, as well as a laundry area, two toilets, and a large linen closet of sorts.

North of the courtyard, curving around Moftakhar Street, was the almond grove, the pomegranate orchard and two clusters of

---

[3] *Azi Dahaka*: three-headed Avestan dragon
[4] *hammam*: Middle Eastern steam bath

apricot trees, all linked together by a single gravel path. Sweet and sour cherry trees lined the entire back garden walls, providing ample privacy for Asqar Aqa and his wife, should they feel inclined to frolic under the blossoms come springtime.

The garden culminated in what was later dubbed Mehdi's pigeon house, a mosaic pavilion that matched the courtyard fountain. Featuring only the whitest of Persian pigeons, the pavilion was enclosed by flowerbeds, which changed according to whatever lady's tastes were running the household at the time. Under Mahin Banu's reign, any flower or plant with a white or silvery cast to it, that could compete with the white of the pigeon plumes, was permissible—milky buttercups, snow-white peonies, and the fairest of climbing poet's jasmines, all serenading the quivering pigeons with their sweet, perfumed couplets.

The Mouse in the Chest

Mahin Banu had a black but lustrous imagination which, unlike her static coiffures, ran windswept and untamed. One afternoon, when Asqar Aqa came home from work for his daily lunch-break and siesta, he noticed his wife was missing. He searched everywhere around their labyrinth of a house calling, 'Mahin! Mahin!' but she was nowhere to be found. He called his mother, who lived with the couple, as any widowed Persian mother would.

'Khanum Bozorg, where is Mahin?'

But the old woman only answered, 'I don't know. She was just here. Perhaps she is in her room.'

Asqar Aqa stuck his head into Mahin's tapestried room, where his wife could often be found playing with her jewelry collection, like a greedy, meticulous little bowerbird, but still found no sign of her. Once his hunger really began to kick in, he decided it would be best to go into the kitchen and help himself to some of the rice and *khoresht*[5] that was already heated on the stove and wait for his wife to come home from wherever she had gone. He sat down in the sitting room with his silver tray, but before he could get the first bite in, he heard a *tick, tick, tick* sound coming from a

---

[5] *khoresht: various meat and vegetable stews in Persian cuisine, poured on top of rice dishes*

large wooden chest in the corner of the room. He peeked in, in case there was a mouse hiding out in there. But there was no mouse. No, there was just a Mahin, barely conscious in the chest, gasping for air. Asqar Aqa, dumbfounded at finding his wife inside the sitting room furniture, helped her out and said, 'Mahin, what the hell are you doing in there?'

And Mahin Banu began to wail. She had worked herself up all morning to the idea that if she were missing, her husband would bring another woman home. Having experimented with hiding in several different places after her morning tea, she had decided that the sitting room chest was her best bet, as it afforded a perfect view of the centrally located front corridor. Unfortunately, once she got in there, she couldn't pry the lid open again from the inside and was stuck in the damp box all day with hardly any air.

After hearing her confession, Asqar Aqa gave a flickering laugh and cuddled his wife, whose current state of hysteria was not of the ceramic variety that would have come crashing in against his embrace.

'Are you crazy, my love?' he smiled, cupping her face in his hands as if he were about to drink her. 'Why would I bring another woman into my home, where my wife and my mother and everybody else live?' This, what he considered, logical explanation, seemed to open up new coffers of doubt in Mahin Banu's imagination. All too familiar with the mad white elephant that charged across her already exaggerated eyes at such times, Asqar Aqa quickly changed tactics. He spent the rest of the afternoon at home, reassuring his young wife at random intervals that there were absolutely no other women, that Mahin Banu was the only girl he ever loved in his life.

Baby Bites

Mahin Banu was notorious for having a short, hairy sort of temper, crowned with just a little bald spot of crazy. When her second daughter, Shuku, was only a baby, and whined and whimpered and complained, as babies do, Mahin Banu would softly bite her on her tiny, shish-kebab arms, just to get the tears out, as she put it. There was a time she bit little Shuku so hard, that the child's purple screams looped around the entire house, up the stairs, into the courtyard, and all the way through to the almond grove, where Asqar Aqa's mother lay snoring after having raided the fuzzy *chaqaleh badooms*[6] all day.

Disgruntled from having been woken up by the child's shrieks, Asqar Aqa's mother ran into the basement, only to find Shuku all by herself, her little white arm already coated with a thick ring of bruises and speckled with saliva. There was no doubt in her mind that this was Mahin Banu's work. She reproached her daughter-in-law, who upon finding that her bite had affected such shrieks, had snuck away to the other end of the house.

'You're crazy! Your temper, it's out of control! She's only a baby!' And with that, she collected Shuku in her scarves, spoiling her for the remainder of the day with pretty white muslin dresses, rice cookies and strings of teeny tiny pearls.

November 1943

'I don't want this one,' Mahin Banu told her miniature mother over tea. She was pregnant with her third child and was convinced it would be another girl. How she knew she was bearing a daughter, nobody knows. But whether it was a conclusion she drew based on old wives' conjectures or purely instinctual, Mahin was right.

'You have no choice,' her mother declared plainly, sucking on a sugar cube. 'Just wait and pray and you'll see. Perhaps it will be a boy.'

But Mahin knew the truth. When she found out that her first child, Homa, was a girl, she cried ruby pomegranate tears in the pomegranate orchard. When Homa died of a bad case of meningitis, Mahin Banu had Shuku and cried for weeks in circles around the courtyard fountain. This time, though, this third time, Mahin Banu resolved to cry no more.

'This is a girl,' she said, 'and I don't want her.'

Skulking around in every dark corner of the house, she downed various potions and folk remedies, in the hope that she might induce a miscarriage.

---

[6] *chaqaleh badoom:* tart, unripe almond consumed in the spring as a delicacy

For six months she tried. She consumed bizarre concoctions like cooked turmeric powder and castor oil, which besides making her vomit did nothing much else. She stuck great egret feathers into her body, in order to pierce the womb and break her water. She rubbed opium around her labia to try and poison the fetus. Everything the floral headkerchiefed women and bearded witch doctors told her to do, she did. Still, the baby would not die.

'I will not let go,' it hummed, from the depths of her belly.

Mahin Banu bit her nails until the pinks of her fingertips tingled. In one final attempt to get rid of her child, she called on a notoriously fraudulent herbal doctor who lived in the southern slums of Tehran. Short, sharp and decrepit, with worm-eaten teeth and abominable breath, the charlatan herbalist prescribed mysterious disk-shaped tablets, which he ordered Mahin to dissolve in water and drink daily.

'If you see yourself bleeding,' he told her, 'make sure to flush the remaining pills and the prescription down the toilet. I assure you, this will be the end of your baby.'

Mahin followed the doctor's orders that night. She plopped the gigantic tablets into her water and drank the fizzy, white brew. When she woke up the next morning, her face had puffed up to twice its normal size and turned sickly yellow.

Every visitor that came to see the family for the next two days, noticed the sudden physical alteration in the ordinarily moon-faced young girl, asking uneasily, 'Mahin, what has happened to you? Why is your face that color?' to which she could only muster some feeble excuse.

On the third day, Mahin Banu saw blood. Adhering to the doctor's counsel, she flushed the wrinkled prescription and leftover tablets down the toilet. All evidence was now safely disposed of.

Within moments of swilling the last pills away with the ewer, Mahin's water broke. Blood began to pour onto the blue mosaic floor, drenching the tips of her hair as she collapsed onto her side. Hearing her dark, conch screams, the Moftakhar family rushed to the outdoor toilet.

Although alarmed that she was giving birth at only six months and that she was hemorrhaging badly, the family figured she was just in labor and clenched their hands for the best. Having no knowledge of Mahin's secret schemes nor of the poison she'd been ingesting for the past three days, they called her legitimate physician and carried her into her room where, despite all her efforts, she gave birth to a baby girl.

Her attempts to poison the fetus had failed. Mahin absorbed the entirety of the poison herself, whilst the baby miraculously separated from her mother's body. She came out teeny and premature but sturdy as a little stone. Mahin herself did not survive. She died that November, at the age of nineteen, on some sheets and newspapers in her bedroom.

The Persian Princess and the Pea

Dank silhouettes of the recent events lingered for some time in the Moftakhar household. Aware of the chaos that was sure to ensue, Mahin Banu's eldest sister took it upon herself to hide the newborn baby in a safe place. Some mute corner where she would not be stirred by the hordes of rocking mourners or passed along dismal, sopping hands.

Like a hasty embalmer, Khaleh Bozorg padded the baby with cotton, wrapped her up in a few sloppy layers of gauze and stowed her away in an oversized closet. The closet, lurking glumly in the remote, eastern-most end of the house, was where the family kept its summer beds and blankets, as well as any additional linen. A *korsi*[7] stood in the center of the room, stacked to the ceiling with a leaning tower of guest mattresses. On the pinnacle of this tower slept Mahin Banu's baby.

Adhering to tradition, the Moftakhars and Samenis grieved for three unbroken days. At the end of the third day, the murder of crowing mourners adjourned, leaving the immediate family to itself until the seventh day, at which time they would be sure to return with empty bellies.

As the last guests caravanned home, Asqar Aqa and his mother, previously occupied with the loss of Mahin Banu and the spectacles of funeral, suddenly realized they had not seen the baby in three days.

---

[7] *korsi: traditional Persian furniture, similar to a low table. In the winter, a heat generator fueled by coal, gas, or electricity is placed underneath the korsi and a stuffed comforter is draped over it. Individuals or families then gather around the korsi on the floor, stretching their legs underneath the comforter for warmth.*

'God strike us down, where is the baby?' they cried, searching frantically around the house, while Khaleh Bozorg was nestled at home under her own *korsi*, deep in a seventh sleep. Resigning to the dark notion that the baby was lost for good, the entire family continued its search despondently until morning, when Khaleh Bozorg finally called.

'God have mercy,' she cried, ripping at her skin. 'I left the baby on top of the *korsi* in the closet!'

The family was delirious. 'But we've pulled at least a dozen mattresses from in there, for all the guests!' they howled.

It was true. Every distant relative, far-flung friend, and dejected neighbor that had come to pay their respects to the family, ended up staying at least one night at the Moftakhar house. And with each visitor, some housekeeper or self-delegated welcome committee of irrelevant women, had set off to the closet and pulled a mattress from underneath the cringing pile.

The family stampeded to the east end of the house.

'The little baby must have suffocated by now!'

'Poor baby, in there for three days! Poor thing must be dead!'

They surrounded the closet, which was looking a lot more jovial these days, and flung open its rickety door. Half a dozen mattresses were still piled up on the *korsi*. But no baby lay on top.

'She is gone!' Khaleh Bozorg was stunned.

'Did somebody steal her?'

'Stand away from the light.'

'How could she disappear?'

'Perhaps her mother summoned her back,' Asqar Aqa concluded miserably, tears welling up in his droopy eyes. He was neither spiritual nor religious, but suddenly found himself in desperate need of a supernatural explanation.

'Don't be ridiculous,' his mother interjected. 'Either somebody moved her, or she is in this room.'

'Wait...over there in the back. What's that over there?' someone called out.

'It looks like a pillow.'

'Oh, I think that's mine,' a thieving neighbor insisted.

But it wasn't hers. Behind the heap, wedged in a two-inch space between the *korsi* and the wall, was Mahin Banu's baby. Silent and poised, with ample patience to spare, the tiny bundle had been lying there for three days now. Her enormous black eyes glared confidently at the stupefied Moftakhar family, who pulled her out and inspected her in the sunlight, among the mocking dust flecks.

'Her destiny must be to stay in this world,' they all agreed. 'And we should not let her die.'

Asqar Aqa's mother laughed. It was the first laugh they had all heard in days and looked odd against the blackness of their clothes. She took the baby in her arms, gave her a dry, wrinkled kiss and asked, 'So why is it that you want to stay in this world so bad, huh, you little turd? Tell me, what is it that you plan on doing here, that you hang on to dear life with such tenaciousness?'

Mohtaram Khanum

Mohtaram Khanum lived in the small, religious city of Ray, commonly referred to as ShahAbdolAzim, just on the outskirts of Tehran. Home to the shrine of the Shiite martyr, Shah Abdol Azim, the city attracted masses of pilgrims every year, each with their own pocketfuls of prayers and fistfuls of wishes.

Mohtaram Khanum herself did not pray, did not wish. She was a hardworking, sensible woman who from an early age had learned to accept all the mud and holes and meatless days of her poverty. She did not cry when her husband drowned late that winter in the public *khazineh*[8], leaving her pregnant and alone with four children, under a crumbling roof of brick and mortar. Instead, she stuck pots and jars under each soggy spot and, having no radio or phonograph, listened to the mystic ghazals of the evening rain, until the dry season. Nor did she cry when her baby died only a month after its birth. She watched the men bury the newborn in silence and devised a plan to patch the roof up in the forthcoming months.

Rarely did any of Mohtaram Khanum's wealthier relations visit ShahAbdolAzim. Occasionally, her mother's sister, who worked as a cook in the Moftakhar house, stopped by with food staples or money or employment opportunities. But the Moftakhars themselves had only once set foot in their forgotten

---

[8] *khazineh: small but extremely deep pool of boiling water, previously used in public hammams for religious cleansing*

cousin's leaking abode. Until, late one November, Asqar Aqa appeared at her doorstep.

He was carrying the usual parcels of fruits and sweets that Mohtaram Khanum's aunt would have delivered on such a visit, but a more peculiar parcel lay cradled in his arms.

Mohtaram Khanum invited her distinguished guest inside and offered him some of the tea and dates that he had brought along. She used her best tea set—clear, delicate glasses, each glazed with a faded gold rim—and assessed the brew in the sunlight, ensuring that it boasted the dark henna color of a good Persian tea. After some polite chitchat over the general state of things, brief but genuine mutual condolences and some not-so-genuine cooing on Mohtaram Khanum's part over what was essentially a weak, sickly-looking baby, Asqar Aqa finally laid out his offer.

'I will help you out in any way I can, Khanum,' he began, with a slightly uneven voice. 'But it is I who am left at your mercy. My mother has been feeding this child sugar water for two days now. But she cannot, will not, survive like this.'

If Mohtaram Khanum had been the praying type, she would have set off to Shah Abdol Azim's mirrored shrine that very day, showering his tomb in gratitude with her roof savings. But as she was not, she kept her money, took the baby in her arms and, once Asqar Aqa left, nursed her with what should have been her own baby's milk.

For two years, Mahin Banu's baby remained nameless in ShahAbdolAzim under the care of Mohtaram Khanum. In these two years, she caught every major disease in the city—chicken pox, measles, mumps, typhoid fever. She got them all, and Mohtaram Khanum nursed her through them all.

On Fridays, Asqar Aqa visited his daughter, taking care that the child's wet-nurse never went hungry. At first he came alone, lugging bags full of stone-baked bread, lamb and syrupy sweets for the children. Two weeks later, he brought Mahin Banu's youngest sister, Mehri, along with him. Three weeks later, the Samenis began urging Asqar Aqa to marry Mehri. Four weeks later, he did.

By the last time Asqar Aqa returned to ShahAbdolAzim, ready to welcome his daughter home, Mehri had already given birth to two children and was pregnant with her third. And of course, as fate would have it, all three of them were boys.

Although Mohtaram Khanum did not cry when Mahin Banu's scrawny, dark child finally left her home, she did visit the Moftakhars twice a month for the next sixteen years, reminding them each time, 'That's my child. She drank my milk for two years.'

For Name's Sake

Every woman who married into the Moftakhar family was given a *laqab,* or descriptive title, which replaced however common or glorious a past she might have had in her father's household with the sugary indulgences and saffron luxuries of her husband's home. Over the years, as the young Moftakhar bride blossomed into womanhood, she learned how to adjust her personality to fit her newly embroidered name. She exposed previously veiled qualities, taking care to exaggerate her most valuable assets. She drew attention away from traits which no longer suited her, disguised her various shortcomings. And wherever there was space, she squeezed new parts in.

It was thus that the already crinkle-browed Ezat lifted her chin an extra two centimeters, raised her shoulders an extra four, and assumed all the lofty airs of Ezat Zaman; that the virginal Batul dropped her black scarves and twirled in the antique moonlight of Mahin Banu; that the lemon-breasted Ozra ripened into the fertile, cosmic beauty of Mehr Afaq; and that the slight, silent Fatemeh, hitherto hidden in the dim corners of her father's home, boldly emerged into the fat, cackling sunbeams of Furuq Azam.

Asqar Aqa knew that his own daughter's name was also likely to only be temporary, so he hardly protested when the scrunched man at the registration office said, 'Zohreh? That's not an Islamic name. You should give her an Islamic name.'

'An Islamic name? Like what?'

'Well, I have a list right here.' He took out a booklet with a handful of names scribbled inside. 'Let's see. There's Belqeis, Fatemeh, Khadijeh, Sakineh, Kolsum....'

'Oh, just pick one.'

'Hmmm. Okay. How about this one?' He held up the booklet in the air.

Asqar Aqa rubbed the inner edges of his eyes with his thumb

and forefinger, dragged the two fingers down around his mouth, focused on the page and frowned. '*That* one? Really?'

'And why not?' the clerk dared. 'One Islamic name is as good as the other.'

Asqar Aqa consented and was in fact quite happy with himself, until he came home with the baby's papers later that evening.

'You named her *what*?' His mother looked at him in craggy disgust. 'Wasn't there an uglier name there for you to choose?'

'Eh...what do you want me to do about it now?'

'Really, we send you to do one thing and you come back with... *that*.'

'Maybe we can call her Zohreh at home?' Asqar Aqa suggested.

'Akh, no.' Khanum Bozorg waved him away. 'You helped enough already. Zohreh, Zohreh,' she mimicked, then turning to her new daughter-in-law, 'We'll just have to find something that rhymes with her sister's name for her.'

'What rhymes with Shuku?' Asqar Aqa asked.

'Niku,' Mehri said.

Claire Morton
from *The Toadstone,* a novel

Chapter One

Standing outside the undertakers, on a dim September afternoon, Lily forgot about the wedding and her parents' relentless questions. She'd walked away from their house to escape that commotion, and had ended up at the funeral parlour, wondering if Sam Wilson's dead mother was as beautiful as she remembered. She hovered outside the door, unsure whether she ought to go in. But after a while her curiosity coupled with the cold, encouraged her to push the door open.

The room was simple, a few low chairs and a desk, behind which stood a man in a stiff suit and an unassuming smile.

'Are you here to see Patricia Morel?' he said. The strange name left Lily unable to answer. She knew her as Trish, the surnames she could never remember.

'Yes,' she replied.

'When you're ready, you can go through to the private viewing room,' he said, his businesslike manner making the scene feel usual. He led her to the door beside the desk and his hand pushed down on the handle. 'There's someone in there now, but please,' he whispered, as he opened the door and ushered her inside.

The coffin lay open on a cloth-covered stand at the back of the small room. A flower arrangement and some lit candles were positioned on a table, but other than that there were only two chairs. Two chairs and now, two people, who had not seen each other for ten years.

He had his back to her, leaning over the head of the coffin. He was much bigger than she remembered, though the blond curls made her certain it was Sam. The door clicked shut behind her before she could withdraw from the room. She thought if he hadn't heard her, she could back out silently. Reaching for the handle, her heel tapped the floor tile and he glanced over his shoulder at her.

'Sam?' she said, and he stared vacantly into her face as she approached him. Except for the three deep lines across his forehead and the hollows beneath his eyes, he hadn't changed much. She touched his elbow with her hand. He looked at her, his eyes shielded by a thick surface of tears as he searched her face. Feeling older and unsuitably smart in her heels, she became uncomfortable, aware that she might look different to him. Her hair was darker and she worried that he might not know her; that she'd have to introduce herself in the room with a corpse. He looked lost, a mess of emotions clinging to his limp hair and loose clothes. Twisting his features into life as he recognised her, he blinked and two tears dropped down onto his jacket.

'Lily?' he said, and clutched her thin shoulders, pulling her towards him. In his embrace she could smell the damp wool of his jumper and feel the pulse in his neck where her ear pressed against it. She prised herself from his grasp to look at him.

Panic bubbled beneath the surface of her calm expression. She felt unexpectedly needed. As she looked at him now, he seemed helpless and pathetic, an old friend she had long pushed from her memory, suddenly desperate. Sam loosened his hold of her and wiped his nose and eyes with his sleeve.

He looked away from her, saying quietly, 'I'm sorry. I didn't expect to see you.' He inhaled deeply, while she waited. 'I mean I hoped you'd come for the funeral, but I...'

Lily, unsure what to say, recalled the black suit of her father's hung over the kitchen chair in dry cleaner's cellophane, a phone call from the florist for her mother, and the words 'Poem for Trish' on the notepad in the kitchen. These things had seemed unreal to her, and been brushed aside on her arrival, everyone preferring to focus on the wedding.

She looked into the mahogany coffin, Trish's dark curls spread onto the pleated satin lining. Her skin was a flawless white. It clung to her face in a smooth mask except for the few thin lines around her eyes and mouth, the side-effects of always smiling. But this was not the Trish she remembered. This woman had her eyes closed and Lily tried to remember if they were green or brown. The body was motionless beneath her thin blue dress. Lily couldn't comprehend that.

'When, when is...?' she said, and swallowed the remainder of the sentence, 'I'm so sorry.' She touched him again and goose-pimples raced each other up her arm and spread across her back and neck.

'Thursday,' he said. 'Jon has made the arrangements for Thursday. Your parents have told me they're coming.'

'Yes,' she said. She held her breath as the silence grew between them and the awkward moment extended itself into minutes. Lily couldn't think of a way to leave. She knew there were things she should say, apologise for, but none of that seemed appropriate now or here. 'Let's go and get a coffee,' she said.

'No…I really…'

'Please,' she said.

Sam nodded and looked into the coffin once more before she guided him out.

She ordered two coffees and sat next to him so that they could both look out the window. She found that men talked more if she did not look at them, but sat by them, listening, and so she assumed this pose with Sam, her oldest friend, as if he were a lover and they were sifting through issues.

A man and his son walked past outside, heading for the post office. The boy clutched an A4 envelope with one hand and with the other held the man's hand. The Indian woman who ran the corner shop overtook them, her legs moving quickly along the pavement. A breeze shook the cherry trees and sent the blossom to stick to the cars that had formed a traffic jam from the T-junction further along the road, while Sam and Lily sat in silence a little longer.

After a minute or two of his staggered breathing, he folded onto the table. 'I've been a bad son, Lily,' he said in a whisper, looking up at her.

'Don't be ridiculous,' she said, leaning in and adopting his quiet tone.

'I was impatient with her,' he said. 'I didn't even go to the last wedding.' The word 'wedding' rang out, filling the gap in their conversation while the waitress put their coffees on the table. She reminded Lily of herself, when she worked here as a teenager, and though the girl wasn't as tall or attractive as Lily, she was pretty with the blonde hair that Lily naturally had. He continued, 'She said I was being unsupportive. She was right, I was. I was so selfish. I just couldn't believe in her anymore. It's impossible to believe that a woman can be in love that many times. Sebastian is barely ten years older than us.'

He stirred his coffee with the teaspoon so that it scraped round the sides. Lily sipped hers quietly, holding her cup in her left hand. Noticing that her engagement ring had swivelled round again, she felt the diamond pressing into her hand against the cup. The coffee shop was full of mirrors and the light caught and reflected itself around the room. She couldn't see Sam in any of them.

'Maybe she was lonely,' said Lily.

'How could she be lonely? She was always around people. She was fifty-five and partied like she was twenty.' A waiter steamed milk behind the coffee machine for a man at the counter, the frothing noise filling the café. 'I don't know why I'm being so aggressive about it,' he said, 'I just never understood her and now I never will.' His eyes glazed over again and Lily felt his grief.

She didn't have the right words, so she extended her arm around his lower back and laid her head on his shoulder. Her hand and arm felt warmed by the skin beneath his shirt and he smelled warm too, manly, but without the vinegary strength of men's aftershave. This was *his* odour she could smell and she felt at home near it. She stayed there, comfortable, listening to him breathe. Sam leant his cheek on the top of her head and put his arm around her shoulder, his face very close to hers. She was aware of how they must look to passers-by. Feeling his lips on her hair, she let his faltering breaths wash over her.

He said, 'So how've you been? I haven't seen you since...'

'I really like this place,' she said, 'it's nice and light.' She shifted a little away from him and sipped the coffee, not wanting to talk about the wedding and not quite sure if he knew about it. She was happy consoling him, being the friend she should have been.

'Remember when this place first opened?' he said. She didn't look up. 'We came here with your Dad, remember?'

'Oh yeah,' she said. 'We must have been about ten.'

'No, older, I think, because we weren't at Holy Trinity anymore.'

The mention of her old primary school made her laugh. Her face broke into a broad smile, showing Sam a perfect set of white teeth as she threw her head back a little.

'You had that silly watch on. The huge one that used to be

Richard's and it slipped off into your ice cream,' she said, while Sam rolled up his sleeve. 'And you spent ages wiping it and moaning that you felt so bad about it, because it was a present.' She punched his arm lightly in the mocking way of an adolescent.

'What, this watch?' he said, really smiling for the first time since seeing her.

She laughed again, saying, 'It fits you now,' and it looked good on him too. She fingered the metal strap and touched the face of the old watch. Letting her fingers linger over his skin, she could feel his hairs as she drew her hand away.

'I wasn't thinking of that,' he said, holding her in his gaze. 'I was thinking about how you said you'd like to run a café when you got older.'

'Did I?' she said, looking away from him. 'I don't remember. I wonder why I said that.'

'It was a cute dream,' he said, replacing the coffee cup into its saucer.

'Maybe,' she said.

'My mother wanted to do that too,' he said.

'Really? When?' She watched him carefully, unsure of whether she should be steering the conversation towards Trish again.

'When she was with Richard.' His tone told her that he thought this was obvious. Finishing her coffee, she put the cup down next to his. It started spitting outside and they watched the raindrops fleck the window.

'So how's the job? London treating you alright?'

'All fine. Yeah.' It was difficult to elaborate. She had almost completely become someone else since she had last seen him. But here she was, feeling as though she'd never left her home town and never been further away from him than these few inches.

After several minutes of staring into the empty coffee cups, he said, 'I've missed you,' and he placed a slightly moist kiss just above her eye.

She looked at him. 'Missed you too,' she said, feeling a stab of pain in her abdomen and a tightening in her chest.

Lily declined another coffee from the waitress and asked for the bill. Sam emptied his pocket into his palm the way Lily remembered him doing as a boy. He sorted through the change for a while and then put the coppers and crumpled tissue back. He got out his wallet and stared inside it a while, then began slowly closing it again.

'Here,' she said to him, putting a five-pound note on the silver tray. 'My shout.'

He squeezed her shoulder as they got up, 'Thanks Lily,' he said. 'It was great seeing you. And I'm sorry.'

'Don't be sorry,' she said, pressing her fingertips into his chest, 'but don't forget you owe me a coffee.' She smiled and then stopped smiling. Unsure why she'd been unable to mention the wedding, she turned on her heel and left him again.

Chapter Seven

I didn't see Lily so often once Mum had decided to sell Richard's place. We hadn't moved far away, but neither of us could be bothered to cycle or walk the extra mile. In the summers though, I always tried to make the effort. One particular day, when the sun had been out for weeks, I went to see her. David was on the scene then, following my mother everywhere she went. He'd given me a fishing rod for my birthday that year as a way of buying his way into our family, and though I wasn't keen on David, I did like the present. I wanted to take a walk down to the river, set up a fishing line and just relax in the shade. Stopping by Lily's, to see if she wanted to come, was just an after-thought.

Her front lawn had just been mown and the grass-cuttings littered the drive bringing the fresh smell of summer into the air. When I rang the bell, no one came and I was just about to turn and go when she opened the door. She was wearing a dressing gown several sizes too small. Its sleeves stopped at her elbows and the length was well above her knees.

'Hi,' she said, smiling as she chewed on her lower lip and looked down at the floor. 'I was just about to get in the shower.'

'Oh...sorry,' I said, feeling embarrassed.

On her doorstep, I found myself staring at her toenails, painted a darker red than my mother's. I'd known her a long time, but even when Molly used to dress her in those ridiculous tunics and plait her wispy hair, I'd never really thought of her as a *girl* before.

Lily was always the scruffy one, boy-like in appearance. But there in the clear sky's sunlight, her golden hair made you want to touch it, to see if it really was as soft as it looked.

'I...er...was just wondering if you wanted to come fishing?' It sounded such a foolish thing to say as she stood there nearly naked, waiting for me to get to the point.

'No thanks, Sam.' She was smiling again when I looked at her. 'Matthew Grange is having a party tonight. Are you coming?'

Matthew lived in Onslow Road, just a street away from Lily's. The same road I'd lived on in Richard's old house. Matthew was a few years older than us, sixteen or so, and his place had a long driveway, two Mercedes and a swimming pool. I'd heard that his parents were in France for the weekend. He'd once got me into a fight on Bracknell High Street. I came off worse with a black eye and a sore hand, while Matthew barely had a scratch.

'I don't know...' I said.

I watched her twirling some strands of hair around her finger, wondering what she would look like at a party. I struggled to picture her out of the jeans and t-shirt she usually threw on, or that uniform with its baggy sweatshirt that made her look like an old woman from a distance. I replayed her words. 'Are you coming?' she'd said, as if she wanted me to go, not 'are you going?' hoping I wouldn't.

'You should,' she continued, 'He said that everyone's welcome.' I watched her fingers touch her neck and slide over her collarbone, slightly covered by the white towelling. She backed into her house, smiling, saying, 'Drink?' and I followed her into the kitchen, still holding on to my fishing rod.

The kitchen had a little breakfast bar, with the fridge under its marble top.

'It's been so hot, hasn't it?' she said.

She was reaching for the orange juice in the bottom of the fridge door, the dressing gown gaping slightly at the neck. She poured two glasses then sat next to me on the other stool. Crossing her legs, she exposed her knee and a slice of her thigh between the parted folds of the garment. Her skin looked smooth and tanned. I drank greedily and must have left an orange smile at the corner of my mouth, because she suddenly laughed. It was a new laugh, one I hadn't heard before, higher and with less feeling. She leaned towards me and with her fingers, touched my lips. The smell of coconut made me want to breathe her in, but the sound of a car turning into the drive broke the spell. I shifted, uncomfortably, as she wiped my cheek, like a child cringing at his mother keeping him from play.

She finished her drink while I watched Molly and Joseph unloading various plants from their car.

'So you're not coming tonight?' she said with an element of disdain.

'No, I don't think I will, but thanks. I just came round to see if you wanted to come fishing, but you don't, so I'll be off. See you soon.'

My words tumbled over each other. I was making my way out of the kitchen, feeling as though I'd spent all afternoon by the river and come away with nothing.

'Sam, wait!'

She wrapped herself further into the dressing gown, getting up and following me to the front door.

'I mean…I know why you don't want to come. The fight with Matt, I mean. I didn't mean to make you feel bad for not wanting to come.'

'It's fine,' I said.

And it had been as if the whole incident before hadn't happened at all. She became normal again. Herself.

'I really need to get in the shower,' she said.

Watching her run up the stairs, I shouted, 'Yeah. You smell.'

Chapter Nine

Sam just wasn't as interesting once I'd discovered boys. I must have been conditioned to think that boys were supposed to find me attractive, because that's what I remember most about convent school. We'd think about each boy we knew and ask, *does he fancy me?* When the answer was no, we'd ask, *how can I make him like me?* And there was usually scope to twist the situation. So we became like chameleons, changing colour to suit the boys we surrounded. They came in crowds: friends of this girl's brother, that girl's cousin, the Gordon's boys, the Camberley lads. At pool parties or scummy basement flats, we adapted to fit in, wherever. It never mattered to me then, who they were, if I liked them or not. Cynthia and I simply decided which boys we liked and which we didn't according to how many other girls liked them. Boys who were unaffected by our charms were denounced as 'sad' or 'losers' and we'd continue our little game until we either won them over or stopped hanging out with them.

But for a long time, I didn't enter Sam into my mental contest. I didn't try to put him into one of my two categories: boys that fancied me, and boys that didn't. We were close, perhaps closer than I was with any of my new girls' school friends, and at first I didn't want anything to change. It wasn't until we went swimming once, that I became fully aware we were different genders. This was before all those boys, and those games, became part of my life, but it started the ball rolling somehow.

Clouds leaked that day. My dad took us to Coral Reef, one of those pools with water slides and rapids. He gave us some money, dropped us off and said he'd pick us up in a couple of hours. The rain hit the glass roof like an army of angry drums in the foyer. You could smell the chlorine right from the automatic doors and hear the children screaming with delight in the bare corridors. It didn't get weird until we got to the changing rooms. This was the first time we had come on our own. My dad had always come with us before, taking me into the men's changing room with him and Sam. At the men's door we both stopped.

'See you in a bit then,' said Sam, and went on into the changing room.

I had to walk further to where the 'Ladies' sign was pressed into the wall. As I pushed the door a large woman came out, holding her son's hand and I had to move aside so she could pass. The smell of chlorine was stronger, spilling out from the room. Hairdryers masked the squeals of children, running showers muffled ladies' laughter while I found a space to put my bag on a slatted bench. Around me women stood naked, towelling their hair dry, or putting cream on their legs, while children ran around in armbands. I had seen my mother's naked body in the bath, but it didn't occur to me that women would flaunt their flesh to each other in this way. At school we all changed for sport discreetly, each girl facing the wall to dress and undress. I found the changing room fascinating, but was embarrassed by my own immature body. A few girls in my class had recently developed breasts; my own were flat but with puffy, tender nipples. I looked at the woman opposite me on the bench. She had curly blond hair and tanned skin. While I watched her talk to her friend in a breathy voice, she took off her t-shirt and put it in her bag. You could see right through her lacy bra to dark nipples, and she took that off too. Standing there, naked from the waist up with her large breasts flawlessly moulded to her chest, with her slim waist, with her wider hips, I realised the delicacy of a woman's body. Its kind curves and alluring lines made me suddenly, and for the first time, desperate to have them. Later, I learned the word *voluptuous*, and came to associate the word with that woman. But in the changing room, how different our two bodies were, I thought. The woman, who was probably only eighteen, took off her jeans and the knickers that matched her bra. I saw the light brown hair in a small triangle between her legs and looked away, ashamed that I had watched her for so long. Slowly at first, I took off my own clothes, looking around to see if anyone watched me. I stood naked, for a moment, holding my swimsuit in my hands. Cold and feeling like a child, only playing at being a grown-up, I put it on. My pale, straight-up-and-down body was like a boy's; I wanted to trade it for an older woman's.

'You've been ages!' said Sam when I got to the pool. I looked at his body, the same size and shape as mine, and thought, one day he'll look at me the way I looked at that woman.

Of course, once I had decided to add Sam to one my lists, it was pointless. He had always liked me and so teasing him became boring. He would never be one of those boys who asked, 'What's going on?' or 'I thought, you know, that you were *into* me?' not Sam. Sam would never question me, or lose his head over a girl. Instead he would be happy to like me and do nothing. That's what I thought.

William Muir
Little Death

What was her name? he asks me.
   You don't need to know her name. That's not part of the deal.
   I must have a name. I can't picture her without a name.
   My hand in my pocket is clasped round the little compass I carry everywhere. The pointer is broken and no longer indicates north and the glass case is cracked on the front but I have carried this since I was a boy in the belief that as long as I have it, although I may not know where I am going, I also somehow will never be lost.
   I need a name, he persists. You can lie if you want to but this is the only detail you can lie about. Everything else must be the truth.
   The room is dusty, bare floorboards, whitewashed walls coated in dirt. A small wooden chair to sit on. It was Gris who told me about the deal. Last night in the café he mumbled incoherently that I could make some money. It took him three attempts to write the address in my sketchbook before he slid off his stool and fell into an alcohol-induced coma on the floor. Arnaud swept past him and, to much laughter, dusted him down with a broom as he went.
   You can call her Chloe, I say. I think about leaving. I feel uneasy but remember the cupboards are empty. I have no money. It has been six weeks since I left the job and the last painting sold a month ago. The burning orange and yellow landscapes of my dreams have dissipated. There are no more paintings and there is no more paint. My mind is a blank canvas.
   There is silence except for the sound of pen on paper and the rumble of carriages beyond the one small window. Children laughing and shouting, probably returning from school. I wait patiently and look through the metal grille separating me from the man. He is in shadow but seems elderly. A large nose. Tufts of hair surrounding a bald dome. This is about all I can make out. Twenty francs he said to tell a story and I agreed but it was only after I had sat down that he told me what story I had to tell. Normally it would have been fine, but when is life ever normal?

And after what happened, nothing has been normal. I wonder each morning when I open my eyes to a new sun, if anything ever will be again.

He is recording all this but I don't know why or if I should care.

Where did you meet her?

I had a job this summer working for an Italian Merchant. Painting frescoes of his homeland on the ceilings of his apartment in Place de Vosges. A greedy little ball of a man with a beard decorating the bottom of his chin and a permanent sheen of sweat on his forehead. He carried a pocket watch that could have fed me for a year but never once did he leave out even a crumb to feed us workers or a drink to wet our throats. Perhaps his lack of generosity was also the source of his wealth. Although he must have had some form of sentimentality in his heart. Why else would he want to look up and remember the sunlight in Naples while making his fortune in Paris?

He left his apartment at nine every morning and I and my fellow artists would breakfast in the gardens, under the chestnut trees, waiting for him to depart. It was a peaceful time. Coffee and bread. Summer sun. The smell of flowers and grass heavy on the nose. We welcomed the relaxation before the long day ahead lying on our backs on hard wooden boards thirty feet in the air. The ceiling pressed against our faces with Persian Blue and Azure dripping into our eyeballs.

She came by every morning at eight thirty. I could hear her approaching in the quiet of the square. There were six pairs of girls walking in a row and she was always the last one on the right. They wore white linen shirts and black velvet waistcoats, long black skirts and black flat-heeled shoes. They tapped their way towards us led by a stern-looking guardian in a heavy black dress and with more than a hint of a moustache decorating her top lip.

She was a schoolgirl? The man asks, disgust creeping into his voice.

No. A student of music. I believe she was seventeen.

He breathes in a deep breath. I need more detail. What did she look like?

She was just over five feet, sullen looking but with apples in her cheeks that suggested she could smile if you pleased her. Her skin was dark, a luminous raw sienna but with the paleness of the moon somehow running through it. Her hair a rich dark intense black and in plaits that curled round her ears and shoulders. Her chest was flattened by the waistcoat she wore. No jewellery that usually adorns the female form. No earrings, or necklace or rings on her small thin fingers. Straightaway I knew there was something different about this girl. The way she walked, upright, curiously still whilst in motion. The others would stare straight ahead, eyes unfocused, seeing nothing, obviously warned by the guardian to ignore us uncouth men lounging by the benches. But she had her head down. Concentrating on the ground until she was beside me and then she looked. Eyes as black as her hair. Two polished discs of onyx flashed at me under the chestnut trees and she held the look until she had passed and I saw her shine with pleasure at what she had seen.

Day after day I saw her and we held the look a little longer and every now and then she would smile at me through one side of her mouth.

You only ever saw her in the mornings? Never later in the day? Presumably she crossed the gardens on her way home.

I saw her once in the afternoon when I was returning from fetching some brushes from a dealer in the Marais.

Did she smile at you?

I could picture the moment our shoulders brushed against each other. She was busy chatting to the girl next to her and she had turned to see who had touched her. She smiled a big smile, then her cheeks flushed and she quickly looked away. Startled by her unguarded reaction.

Sort of.

The man coughs. A smoker's cough, thick with tar, ending in a rasping sound in his chest before we return to the sound of his pen scratching the paper. But you never went back to the gardens at that time again to hang around in the hope of seeing her?

No. I shift in my chair, more from the ripple of nerves in my stomach flickering through my body than from the unflinching chair on my buttocks. I thought about it, I guess, but it didn't seem right.

Why?

It would have felt as if I was waiting for her.

You were waiting for her already, every morning.

Yes, but I had a reason to be there. In the afternoon... my

voice falters as my tongue grows large and I struggle to find the right words. I would have been acknowledging what was going on. Taking it further. I feel a shadow spinning over me and I shudder.

What was going on? How were you feeling?

You asked for a story, not for my feelings.

Aren't your feelings part of your story?

They are incidentals, not details.

A flame sparks through the grille and his face is momentarily lit in yellow and blue. The face is round with heavy jowls covered in tiny silver hairs. A round red nose flattened as though pressed against a pane of glass. Eyes small glass beads. The sulphur from the match hangs in the air as he sucks in smoke and exudes a cloud into the returning gloom. I can hear church bells ringing, calling the Left Bank to prayer.

Then you must continue with the details.

Two weeks went by at the beginning of September when she failed to appear. I guessed she must have a holiday but deep down, every morning I felt a little more anxious and a little more foolish until I realised that reason had been abandoned when it came to this girl. The trees were turning gold and I started to believe I would never see her again but then she came back. I heard the tap of their footsteps and my chest burst with the sun and I smiled as wide as the Seine as she passed, but there was nothing. Her stride became quicker and her haste to avoid me almost carried her into the back of the girl in front of her. She kept her eyes firmly on the ground, rooted to the cloud of dust created by the soles of her shoes slipping on the gravel and I could sense a tension within her.

It was the same the next day and the day after. I stood helplessly wondering what I had done to displease her but unable to ask her what had gone wrong.

I look at the man peering at me through the grille. It sounds stupid doesn't it? He says nothing. Such worry about a girl I hadn't exchanged one word with.

But it changed, didn't it?

Yes. On the fourth day she looked at me without a smile then looked at the ground and back up quickly and I saw that she had dropped a small square of paper at her feet. I picked it up as the rows of girls disappeared. The note asked me to meet her at midday by the fountain in the middle of the square.

You must have been delighted. A girl so pretty, a girl you liked so much, asking to meet you.

I was at first, but then I became worried. After all she hadn't even looked at me in days.

Is that the only reason you were worried?

The shadow deepens in my soul. I don't know, I reply.

There is a pause and we sit for a while with the noise of the day filtering through the window and across the room. I can hear birds and the carriage wheels continue to turn on the cobbles and a woman outside is singing softly, either nursing a child or performing the simple tasks that mothers and wives perform every day. Hanging out washing or pulling vegetables from the small gardens that run across the back of the houses. Food to cook for the family that evening.

And you went to meet her, he says to prompt me.

I told the boss, Lempreinte, who supervised the crew, I had a buyer coming to my studio to look at my paintings. He grumbled a bit but he is a painter too, so he understood. I went home and changed into my one dress-shirt then returned to wait for her at the fountain. She came at noon. Almost reluctantly along the path. Her footsteps getting smaller the closer she got to me. We said hello, quietly, shook hands. It was as if we were being introduced to each other by someone else. She seemed nervous but still managed a smile. I held her hand a little longer than I should have but she didn't pull away. I suggested a stroll through the city to where we could ride the tram to Montmartre. The sun wasn't too hot and the city was at ease with itself. The workers were working and the loitering classes were busy idling in the cafés. She was very shy at first but strangely confident at the same time. Unafraid to say what she meant. Now and then we would dart a look at each other. Grin. She was full of questions. Where did I come from? What did I do? And she listened intently to the answers and every now and then she would give a short nod as if I had her approval. She told me she was studying violin and showed me the rough surfaces on the fingertips of her right hand and the soft skin of her left hand. She smiled and told me now I had seen her imperfections I would have to accept her for who she was, not who I thought she was or who I wanted her to be. She told me she preferred Mozart to Beethoven and ballet to opera but had fallen in love with Puccini after seeing Tosca in the spring.

Her tutor had told her at the end of last term that he had to cancel her afternoon lesson on this day because he had to attend a rehearsal and he asked her to inform her parents that she would be home earlier than usual but instead she had told them she had an additional lesson and wouldn't be home until six. We wandered through the streets and I felt good. Happier than I had in a long time. There was real energy from this girl. We were so engrossed in each other we were oblivious to everything and everyone we passed.

It's an interesting phrase.

What is?

The phrase, oblivious to everything. He pauses and sucks the last remnants of nicotine from the stub of cigarette clamped in his fingers. A man such as yourself, mature, obviously not Jewish, with this young Jewish girl, holding hands, laughing like lovers. He laughs to himself. A laugh that rumbles the nicotine sludge coating his lungs. I am not surprised you attracted attention.

I never said we attracted attention.

But you must have been aware that you did. The fact you were oblivious to everything suggests you were aware there was something to be oblivious of. Tell me the rest, he says before I can respond, but the thought he has planted sinks into my bones and I feel the sickness begin. I know this will be bad for me but I have started on this journey and chosen to sit in this chair and I need the money to eat tonight.

I took her to the boat. Not an actual boat but my studio. A few of us rent space in the boat. We had some bread and cheese and I made hot chocolate. Mme Berenge saw us sitting on the steps in the courtyard. For once, she laughed, you bring a nice girl home, Modi. She is used to the girls coming and going in the boat. Models we paint.

Do you sleep with these girls?

I shrug and wonder how to explain. The oils that start on a palette and in your head then flow through your veins, through your body. The wine, the opium, the girls' eyes that filter into your bloodstream. The paint that becomes flesh. The soft giving flesh of goddesses on canvas… but there are no words to explain this so I simply say yes. I feel his disapproval through the grille.

He writes more and I realise he now knows my name and I curse myself but he smiles at me.

Do not worry, I will not include your name. This record is anonymous. He leans close so I can see his face. Continue.

I asked Chloe if she would like to see my paintings and she said yes. We went upstairs and I showed her my new work, landscapes, but she was more interested in the portraits of the girls. She asked who they were, how I met them? Lots of questions.

I can see her squatting in front of the canvases, looking through the swirls of bodies stretched out in pose. Her cheeks reddening, hands trembling. They're beautiful, she murmured. Will you paint me? The question took me completely by surprise. Her eyes were gleaming. Precious stones mined from a seam deep below the surface of the earth. Her mouth wide and smiling as her shirt rose and dipped with the quickness of her breath.

I picked up some charcoal, some paper and told her to sit on the bed. To take off her waistcoat. The sun poured through the window onto her black hair, created by a myriad of swirls of blue and green. Colours found at the bottom of the ocean. The curve of her neck was a strip of coastline, a scar of sand at the water's edge. My hands traced over the surface of her skin, following the curve of her lips and the straight line of her nose. Her eyes were black-lined tears with wisps of lashes. I undid the buttons on her shirt to the waist as I drew and she did not protest. I pulled the cloth from her shoulders, arched like the dome of a church and she leaned back to pose. We sat held together with our eyes and my hand and I took in all I could see and put it down as a record in front of me. Eventually she knelt down beside me and looked at the image of how I saw her. I love it, she whispered as she lifted her eyes into mine and I knew she had just seen all that was inside my heart.

That moment should be the last moment, I tell myself. I barely hear my own voice as I retell the rest. The first kiss. A soft and gentle kiss. Her lips barely moving. The trace of my fingers against the richness of her skin. The kisses that followed. Each one deeper and more powerful than the one preceding it. The clothes being removed as the sun burned into our bodies. Her short little gasps of breath. Her eyes held firmly shut. The sharp angles and tightness of her youth. My voice deserts me and I can hear the pen scratching across the paper. It stops. Finish, Modi, he says.

These are the parts of life you hide away from, I say.

I know, but you agreed to tell me your story.

I swallow hard and feel the darkness in the pit of my stomach sending shockwaves through my chest alongside the beat of my heart. I was on top of her. Inside her. Her legs were wrapped around me. She was gasping, moaning as we made love. I felt the intensity building inside me. Her eyes were still tightly shutting out the world. Her nails ripped into my skin and she bit hard on my lip, drawing blood as my orgasm tore in between her legs. She cried out. Not a scream of pain. More a moment of realisation and that's when her eyes opened and she looked at me.

And how did she look at you?

I can see her now, her cheeks a dirty red, tears coming from the corners of her eyes, small pearls of teeth coated in my blood. She looked hurt.

You hurt her, didn't you, Modi?

I didn't hit her or do anything wrong. The sickness is rising in my chest. There is a fever coating my forehead. It has been like this ever since. I didn't do anything wrong. It just was wrong.

How did you feel when she looked at you?

I felt like I had died. Something inside both of us died a little that day

For a long time there is silence except for the sounds of the city carrying on as normal as cities always do. War, pestilence, floods and fires, cities somehow manage to survive.

You haven't seen her since, have you?

No. She gathered up her things and left without saying a word. She never came back through the park. The guardian wouldn't speak to me and I got nothing from the music school. Five days later my boss Lempreinte informed me my services were no longer required. I knew he had heard something. Maybe from the girl's family because he could barely look at me and when he did it was with disgust. He wouldn't answer any questions, just told me never to come back.

The man eyes me through the grille. On the days before you slept with this girl, the days when she ignored you, you know why she ignored you, don't you?

Because she was worried her parents would discover she was

lying.

No, Modi. She was building up her courage to approach you. To write a note asking you to meet her. She was preparing herself to trust you. He sighs and sits back in his chair. She trusted you Modi. I hear a rustle of notes and he sits forward again pushing a twenty franc note along the counter between us. Sliding it under the grille. I reach out and pick up the money.

As promised, he says.

As I stand the sickness rushes into my mouth and my stomach contracts. I clamp my teeth together and my hand grips the money as I steady myself. I breathe in slowly.

He looks at me briefly and waves his hand dismissively. You can go, we're done.

I turn to walk out then turn back. Why do you record these stories? Is it to find out the badness in men's hearts?

He looks startled, as though he has been accused of something he is not guilty of. I teach at the University and I am writing an oral history of the life of the city and the people who live in it. I ask for all kinds of stories. This is part of my research. The answer to your question is no, but as with any research the results aren't always what you expect them to be. He stares at me, then he smiles a matter-of-fact smile. I am not a judge, just a recorder of facts, and neither am I a priest. He runs his fingers across the grille that has separated us. This is not a confessional. I've just found it helps people talk.

Outside, the sun has fallen and there is a sense of night in the air. A chill that makes me shiver. People in the streets are huddled within themselves. Anticipating home or a café. A meal and a glass of wine. I drift beneath the row of electric stars created by the prematurely lit streetlights until I realise I am heading towards the riverbank. I lean over the railings and stare into the surface of the water, stained black with oil and dirt from the barges ploughing their way upstream, belching black fumes into the lilac night. I can see figures on the boats standing atop mounds of coal and twisted iron. The people are staring at me as they sail on, eyes boring into mine. Someone waves at me or the city and I wave back. I put my hands in my pockets. In my left is the twenty-franc note, in the right is my compass. I remember my father watching me unwrap the present in the dining room. A room that was only used for guests or special occasions. The family gathered round the excited little boy tearing the paper packaging from the gift. To show you the way ahead in all your adventures in life, he had said, to show you the way to Elysium. This makes me smile and I remember summer days in the fields, running through the wheat with the sun beating down. My compass held in front of me as I ran and my father laughing at the sight of his son sprinting ahead to find the fields of Elysium. Of course as a child I had fallen, slipped on a stone and the compass had been broken. Somehow as a boy it hadn't mattered. Somehow I knew it would still serve its purpose. I take one last look at the compass and throw it high into the air. It arcs away from me and lands in the river with barely a ripple.

I spin round and walk away as the hunger strikes my belly.

Gris is in the café, hunched over a table. A girl I haven't seen before is sitting next to him. Blonde ringlets and a white shirt rolled at the sleeves. She has her arm round his shoulders and her face buried in his neck.

He raises his head as I take a seat and his eyes are thin, opaque like the membrane peeling away from a new-born calf as it emerges from the womb. His features are broken. It reminds me of Lempreinte telling me to leave. Something has horrified him.

You know, don't you, I say. You know what happened.

He nods and I look away and wonder what I can say.

Who can believe it? He whispers. Capron told me at lunchtime. Told me as if commenting on the weather. Paul is dead and it is raining again.

It takes a few moments for the words to make sense to me and I see a shadow of Paul sitting in the corner as he always did, grinning and laughing. Paul is dead?

Yes. You didn't know? He died October twenty-second. Arnaud puts a bottle on the table, two new glasses and I pour. Gris holds his glass high in the air. The girl is still hiding in the harbour of his neck, refusing to surface. Paul Cézanne is dead and the world carries on without stopping to notice. He knocks his glass against mine. I came here with a dream, Modi. A vision in my head of a new world. Sometimes ugly, sometimes beautiful but at least it was new and it was mine. I think we all came here with a vision but look around you now. It's the same old world as before. As if we were never here at all. He drains his wine from his glass. Maybe this is how it always turns out. Maybe there is no other ending.

    I close my eyes as Gris pours from the new bottle. I try to picture the wheat fields I used to run through, hear my father laughing, the landscapes I used to dream about, but there is nothing but white. Sheer white. My mind is a blank canvas. Except for the girl, in the distance, her back to me as she walks away in silence. I wait for her to look back. Until this happens Gris is correct. I open my eyes and pick up my glass. Painting is dead. I drink and take the twenty-franc note from my pocket and lay it on the table knowing we will soon need another bottle.

Rahul Sethi

Maksuda

Maksuda is nineteen.
She cooks lentils five times a week.
Her daughter loves lentils with rice.
A little yogurt on top and she is an angel,
until her bowl is empty.

Maksuda's husband lives in the city.
He's a coolie, she says, *at the station.*
For a year they haven't seen each other,
since their daughter was born.

He sends money twice a month,
whatever is left after rent and food,
enough for her to buy milk for a week.

She's still paying off the loan.
The manager said she'd no right
to paid maternity leave.

She's back at the factory now
working full-time as before,
eight to five, sometimes till nine or ten,
for two cents an hour,
poking needles through cloth.

Rahul Sethi

Mother

When it came time for the sun to appear,
it was nowhere in sight.

The moon was as confused as we were,
spinning this way and that,
looking over her bare round shoulders.
I saw him as he was leaving yesterday, said the moon.
He didn't say anything about being late.

Mother was furious.
There were tons of tasks on her list for the day,
one of them being my brother and I having to till the soil,
for planting the following morning,
and there was no light to waste.

Tying her hair in a knot and lighting candles for the three of us,
Mother set off in the dark to find the sun,
with my brother and me trailing closely behind.

Mother gracefully raced through the forest
and headed east, toward the sea.
Her morning dress gathered mud round the hem
as she ducked and juked under and around thick brush and branches.
She hopped over puddles and on stones to cross swamps and ponds.
She rarely looked back to see us lagging behind, gasping for breath.

When we reached the sea,
Mother threw away her candle, heaved our rowboat
from the shore onto the waves and jumped in.
My brother and I barely made it into the boat
as Mother began frantically paddling away.

From far into the sea,
we faintly saw a gleam of light on the horizon.
Mumbling curses, Mother paddled faster
as my brother and I shivered and huddled together.

Hidden at the end of the ocean, behind the waves, there he was, the sun,
slouched over and laughing luminously at his devilish prank.

Not amused, Mother grabbed him by the ear
and dragged him across the waves, steaming the sea,
through the forest, lighting fallen leaves,
touching bare branches with flame, to the farm.
Swinging and whipping the sun into the sky,
with clenched teeth and a stern finger, she snarled,
You'd better make sure you stay there till we're done!

Rahul Sethi
Bara Bazaar: God's Market

A crowd circles a tiny stall at a distance from the shop. A metal pole sways a saffron banner with the words *Narayana Sweets*, God's Sweets, over the crowd. While the others look at bangles and shawls, I walk over. I stand on my toes and peek over shoulders of people in front. A large glass display filled with sweets sits in the middle of the circled crowd. Two fat women smack, punch and kick a skinny teenage boy, who looks my age. One woman holds a bitten milk cake in one hand, and punches the boy with the other. Crumbs of milk cake cling to the boy's lips as tears roll down his cheeks. The women pull at the boy's torn shirt and hair, to bring him in closer range. The boy's shirt rips more with each pull, showing his dark skin nestled deep in the crevice of his ribs. He closes his eyes, pressing his hands together. The women slap and punch and kick, calling the boy a bastard, a swine. The crowd watches in silence. The boy falls to his knees from kicks to his shin. He pleads, 'Please. I won't do it again.' The women don't stop.

The saffron banner whips. Frames flicker the glory of Hindu Gods. We ignore the images all around; our interest is gripped by two fat women, a boy in tattered clothes, and a bitten piece of God's milk cake.

Rahul Sethi
Shit-Water

We took two cardboard boxes from the basement and threw them over the rusted, mangled green fence sprinkled with snow. Rohit, my elder brother, cradled his hands together to boost me over. I put one foot in Rohit's palms, hopped off the ground with the other foot, grabbed the top of the fence, pulled myself up, straddled the fence, eased my other leg over and jumped off to land belly-first in the snow.

Our cousins, Amit and Summit, came over that day for the weekend. Amit was eleven and his brother Summit was seven. They lived in Markham, right behind Pacific Mall —or China Mall as we called it, because all the shops were owned by Chinese people. The shop-signs were written in Chinese, all the customers were Chinese and the mall smelled like raw fish and new electronics. Amit and Summit used to buy Sega games from the mall for real cheap.

At the time, Rohit was nine, and Sunny and I were the youngest at six. Sunny's Dad, and our Dad, together with our Dads' youngest brother, our grandparents, and all the brothers' wives and children lived together in a two-bedroom house in Scarborough. Our grandparents took one bedroom; Sunny, his baby sister, and his parents took the other. Our Dads' youngest brother and his wife and their baby slept on the couches in the living room, and my parents, Rohit and I slept on sponge-mattresses in the basement.

Beyond the backyard fence of the house, a huge sewer ran across the stretch of homes in the neighbourhood. In the summer the air reeked. In the winter the wretched odour was masked by the freezing cold, and foot upon foot of snow. The sewer had high, steeply slanted walls, like a V, that led down to the bottom where a stream of sewage water flowed through. We called the stream *shit-water*. In the winter time we sledded down the steep walls in any cardboard boxes we could find at our house or any boxes we could find out on the kerb during garbage pick-up. We'd sled down the walls, then roll and kick out of the boxes to stop just before hitting the shit-water. We would race, usually two racers at a time because that'd be all the boxes we'd find, while a judge always stood near the bottom to announce the winner.

After Amit and Rohit helped me, Summit and Sunny get over the fence, they both hopped over in one move. They grabbed the boxes, dropped them in the snow, and, as they always did, they went over the rules before we started playing.

'Okay, two people start at the top and race down at my signal,' said Amit.

'And I'll be the judge at the bottom,' added Rohit. 'Whoever passes me first and stops before hitting the shit-water, wins.'

'And when me and Rohit race,' continued Amit, 'Sunny will be the judge and Summit signals.'

I raised my hand.

Amit and Rohit looked down at me. 'What?'

'What do I do?' I asked.

They shrugged. 'What do you mean?'

'Like, when, when you two race, Summit gets to signal and Sunny gets to judge. Well,' I licked at snot running down my lip, 'Well, what do I do?'

'You watch,' Amit scoffed.

'Yah, yah, you watch,' Rohit agreed.

My eyebrows narrowed.

'Alright, look,' Amit leaned down, 'you drag the boxes back up for the next race, okay?'

'Okay.'

That day, after about an hour or so of races, Amit and Rohit said that we should have a tournament with something at stake. They decided that whoever came in first place would get to boss around whoever came last for the rest of the day. It was already apparent who were the likely losers and winners. It was always either Amit or Rohit who won in anything we played, them being the eldest, and it was always either me or Sunny who lost, us being the youngest. Summit always cruised by unnoticeably in the middle, never coming in first place, or last. It was always Sunny or me who were the slaves for the day, the shoe-cleaners and general chore-doers and butt-kissers and convenience store candy-stealers, after every tournament. But both of us figured it was better to have played and lost than to not have played at all, although we couldn't have explained it as poetically then.

Before beginning the tournament, Amit and Rohit asked if we all agreed to the stakes. 'So you guys know the deal, right?' said Amit, 'The loser has to be the winner's slave for the night.'

'No whining and crying to your moms either,' said Rohit, 'Or you get beats from all of us.'

Sunny and I nodded nervously, while Summit just *Um-hmm*ed.

The races had gone somewhat as I had already expected, though I was still imagining a victory before every race—what it would feel like to be first, to boss around those older than me, telling them to get *me* a glass of grape juice with cubed ice, or make *me* a grilled cheese sandwich shaped like a star. After having lost to Amit, Rohit, and Summit, while sitting next to Sunny in a race for second-last place, staring down the hill that could possibly slide me into slavery for a day, I was now imagining *myself* with a tiny apron around my childish waist, sweating over a stove, flipping star-shaped grilled cheese sandwiches on a frying pan, then chiselling away at a huge block of ice to get a few cubes for a glass of grape juice I must serve to the victor.

Amit had won in the finals against Rohit. It was a close race. Both of them were bumping sleds all the way down the hill. It was when Amit reached out a hand toward Rohit and pushed him by the head, making Rohit's sled wobble and eventually tip over before the finish line, that sealed the victory for Amit. Amit had jumped out of his box just before hitting the shit-water and waved and hollered triumphantly, as Rohit got up and stammered toward him, yelling that it wasn't a fair win. But all Amit said was, 'Hey, we never made a rule against it.' And that was that. Amit was first place and Rohit kept *no pushing* as a rule in mind for next time.

So there we were, Sunny and I at the top of the hill, looking down at the shit-water, our respective imaginations picturing the tasks we would have to perform if we lost; at least I'm sure Sunny was imagining the same. Amit whispered into Rohit's ear and Rohit ran down the hill with a mischievous grin. Amit stood between us; both of us snuggled into our cardboard box sleds, holding tight to the sides of the box. Amit slowly raised his arms, 'Ready…Set…Go!' He dropped his arms and we both frantically scooched our sleds to the edge of the hill and over. I pressed my back to the box and clutched the sides tighter as the box barrelled down the steep hill. Flakes of snow lifted into the air in my cardboard sled's wake. I looked over to see Sunny a box length behind me. Second-last place was definitely secured. I neared the finish line, which was Rohit standing to one side near the bottom of the hill, and as I crossed I tipped the box over and stopped myself before hitting the shit-water. As Sunny was about to cross the finish line, Rohit leaped on top of Sunny while Amit came awkwardly running down the hill towards them, a wicked smile on his face. Amit and Rohit pulled Sunny out of his cardboard box and laid him flat on his back. They were twice his size at the time. Amit had dug his knees into Sunny's arms and Rohit sat on Sunny's legs. Sunny wailed and tried to yank his limbs free. Amit unzipped Sunny's jacket, grabbed handfuls of snow with his gloved hands and stuffed the snow into Sunny's chest, and then zipped the jacket back up. They both grabbed Sunny by the arms and legs and lifted him up like a sack of flour. Sunny cried and kicked as they carried him to the edge of the shit-water. At the edge, they began to swing Sunny, laughingly, while he cried to his Mom. After a count to three, they tossed him in. They laughed and walked back up the hill, where Summit still stood watching silently. As they passed him, Summit, expressionless, ran down toward Sunny. Sunny pulled himself up. His tears mixed with the foamy, slushy, dark green water as they left his eyes.

After dinner, Amit, Rohit, Summit and I sat on the beige, juice-stained couch in the living room, watching Tom chase Jerry all through a house, a construction site, a mall, a hospital and a bowling alley. To Amit and Rohit's surprise, Sunny hadn't mentioned a thing to any of the adults about what the two had done to him. Instead, with a stone face, he said he fell in by accident, and then calmly went upstairs to shower. After eating dinner quietly, none of us noticed that Sunny wasn't sitting on the couch watching *Tom & Jerry* with us. It wasn't until a Visine commercial that Summit and I noticed he wasn't in sight. During the commercials, we both climbed up the stairs, gripping the hand rail as we climbed to the second floor. The door to Sunny's parents room was open a crack. Faint sobs came from the room. We slowly edged the door open. Sunny was sitting on his bed, his knees tucked into his chest, a blanket pulled up to his shoulders, crying soft tears that rolled down his cheek to his chin, dropping onto a blanket decorated with red roses.

Rahul Sethi
Twisted Ankle

Clarkson students, a ton of black kids with mean mugs, pack Clarkson bleachers, booing as we walk into the gym and throwing empty pop cans. It looks like their school is filled with more hoodlums than ours.

'I don't think they like us,' I say.

Mike grins. 'Naw, man. *I* fit right in. I bet you half these niggas is either related to me, or go to my church. It's *you* they don't like. A Paki in a nigga's school.' Mike chuckles. He knocks the basketball loose from my hands. 'And a basketball-playing Paki at that.' He laughs.

Clarkson's principal, a tall man with thick arms, yells at the students in the bleachers, telling them to pick the cans off the floor.

'Shit, what I just say?' Mike points at a cute girl in baggy jeans and a long sweatshirt. The girl waves at Mike from the bleachers. 'That's my cousin Sheila and her friends right there.' A group of girls with tight braids and pink, purple, and blue weaves sit around Sheila. Mike smiles. 'I be right back.'

Clarkson students glare at Mike as his lanky legs jog towards them. Guys in the bleachers stand and cross their arms. They sit as Mike leans to hug Sheila. I pick up my basketball and dribble to our bench.

Our midget team plays first. The junior team plays after us. It's just an exhibition game but Mr. Clark tells us to 'treat it like it counts'. 'The first game sets the trend for the rest of the season boys,' he says. 'So no friggin' around!'

The junior team sits at an empty end of the bleachers. They avoid the stark eyes of the Clarkson student body and ignore the comments made about their mothers and sexual preferences. They sit huddled together, with their backpacks between their knees.

Clarkson boos and curses every time a player on our team touches the ball. Sheila and friends cheer every time Mike gets a pass or makes a basket. When Mike doesn't have the ball, Sheila and friends chant, 'Pass it to Mike. Pass it to Mike. Pass it to Mike.' So we pass it to Mike as much as possible, just to have someone cheering us on.

With ten seconds left in the game, we're up 54 to 52. Clarkson has possession at their end of the court and they have to toss the ball inbounds.

'Full court press!' Mr. Clark yells and Andre, Zorie, Mike, and Tom hover over Clarkson's players. As the centre, I stand at half court to play safety.

Clarkson's bench, our bench and everyone in the bleachers stand to watch.

My heart pounds under my jersey.

'Alright boys, tight D. No friggin' around!' Mr. Clark yells.

The referee whistles and Clarkson's players dodge all over the court to get open for a pass. Clarkson's point-guard gets by Tom and catches a long toss thrown to him. Mike rushes at the point-guard and tries to sweep the ball away. The short point-guard dribbles, ducks under Mike's lanky arm and sprints by him. He charges in my direction and I hunch and move toward him. The point-guard crosses the ball between his legs and jolts to the basket. I follow beside him until we're both under the net. I stretch my arm out and leap as he jumps to shoot.

'Foul 'im!' Mr. Clark shrieks from the bench.

I slap the point-guard's arm. *Smack*. The ball floats over the backboard and the point-guard falls to the floor. The buzzer screams to signal the end of the game.

The Clarkson student body roars.

The referee blows his whistle. 'Foul.' He clasps his wrist, and tells me to spin around. He glances at the number on the back of my jersey. 'Foul, on the shot, number three-zero.' He holds up two fingers, 'Two shots. No added time.' The referee waves the point-guard over.

The Clarkson student body simmers as the point-guard limps over to the free-throw line. 'Let's go, Damien,' someone bellows from the bleachers.

I sit on our bench and sweat. My hands press together.

Damien dribbles in place at the free-throw line. The gym falls silent as Damien stares at the net and gently bends his knees. He slowly lifts the ball past his waist, past his stomach, his chest, his shoulders, neck, face, head, and flicks his wrist as his arm straightens, sending the ball hurling toward the basket. *Swish*.

'Shit!' I throw my towel.

Clarkson cheers and stomps their feet on the bleachers. Clarkson's coach nods his approval. The score board shines 54 to 53.

Mr. Clark clutches his clipboard to his chest.

Mike winks and waves at one of Sheila's friends. He mouths, 'I'll talk to you after the game.'

The referee tosses the ball to Damien. 'Last shot. Alright coaches, if he makes this we go into overtime,' he says. He blows his whistle.

Damien stands at the free-throw line and dribbles in place. He bends his knees. The gym again falls silent. He slowly lifts the ball past his waist, past his stomach, his chest, his shoulders, neck, face, head, and flicks his wrist as his arm straightens, sending the ball hurling toward the basket. *Clank*. The ball springs off the tip of the rim and bounces down court. Our bench howls and jumps.

'Friggin' A!' Mr. Clark shakes his fist and pats the shoulders of the players in his reach. 'Good job boys. A little closer than I'd like the game to be, but good job. Good foul. Way to hit 'im, *Raul*.'

Mike chuckles and pushes me as we leap and laugh. 'Friggin' A man,' he snickers. 'Friggin' A.'

Our midget team sits inside the dark bus, parked in front of Clarkson Secondary, and waits for the juniors to change clothes and load in. The junior team lost against Clarkson, 63 to 49.

Mike and I sit on the worn seats at the back of the bus and make cracks at Sheila's fat friend Shawntai. 'Yo, you see that girl's weave.' Mike laughs. 'Here she is tryin' to tell me she's half Spanish when it look like she got that hair fresh off a horse this mornin'.' He chuckles. 'And the girl can't catch a hint. I told her like five times that I ain't 'bout to give her my number.'

I laugh.

I look up and see three large Clarkson students climbing onto the bus and scanning the players in the seats. 'Where that tall Indian kid?' One of them bellows, his arms too big for his sleeves.

Mike nudges me to be quiet.

I slouch into my seat.

'Where he at? We just wanna talk to 'im,' he says, and stares at the blank faces of our team.

'Where the hell is Mr. Clark and the bus driver?' I whisper to Mike.

Mike stares straight ahead, and shrugs.

'Shit,' I whisper.

'Eh, look. We just lookin' for that Indian kid, alright? That was my little brother that kid hit and now he got a twisted ankle. I just want 'im to say sorry, that's it. Now where the fuck he at? Damien's brother walks down the bus aisle. His wide frame and bulky forearms rub along the edge of bus seats as he walks closer towards us. No one peeps a word.

Mike elbows me and gestures for me to hide under the seat.

I shift and slide. My knees bump the seat in front. I crouch near Mike's feet and try to slide under our seat, but can't bend low enough. I look at Mike, whispering, 'I can't fit.'

He waves a hand, gesturing me to shut-up, while looking forward. 'I think he's inside the school still, in the washroom or somethin'.' Mike says, and pushes down on my head, trying to force me under.

I slap his hand away.

Damien's brother grins, 'Fuck that.'

Mike hits me with the side of his knee.

'We know he ain't in the washroom.' Footsteps slowly approach our seat. 'We saw the kid walk onto the bus.'

Mike pushes my head down, kicks with the side of his foot, and I try frantically to get under the seat, but can't manage to.

'He ain't sittin' next to you is he?' Damien's brother asks.

Shit. Shit. Shit. I mouth. My legs, neck and back ache as I try to bend and arc and crawl under the seat, without success. Mike throws his bag on my head, and moves his legs closer to me. I try to hide behind them, and hold my breath.

The footsteps stop. Damien's brother hovers over us.

'Like I said, he's in the washroom,' Mike says.

Damien's brother lifts Mike out of his seat, picks up Mike's backpack and throws it at him. I look up at Damien's brother from where I sit squashed on the floor, between two bus seats. I smile awkwardly.

Damien's brother grabs me by the collar of my shirt and pulls me up.

'I'm sorry,' I gasp.

He laughs and yanks me to the front of the bus. The other two grab me by the arms and drag me to the door. I tug and jump and try to pull away. Everyone in the bus stands. Only Mike tries to pull the guys off me. Damien's brother grabs Mike by the throat and tosses him onto a seat. 'Sit the fuck down, nigga. This ain't none of your business,' Damien's brother snarls, and yanks me to the doors.

Mr. Clark steps onto the bus. I sigh with relief. He's shocked by the three large Clarkson students dragging me by my arms and shirt. 'What the frig is goin' on here?' Mr. Clark shouts. 'Let go of him right now!' Mr. Clark pulls Damien's brother and the other two off me. 'Get the hell off of my bus before I call your principal!' Mr. Clark scowls at the Clarkson students and points to the door.

Damien's brother kisses his teeth. He punches me in the gut, and shoves me into Mr. Clark. The three guys nudge Mr. Clark and me as they stride to the door, jump out of the bus and run off. I gasp for breath.

'What the hell was that about?' Mr. Clark frowns.

I drag back to my seat. I look at my ripped collar. I had just got this shirt.

'Someone tell me what the hell just happened.' Mr. Clark shouts.

The team jumps to fill in Mr. Clark on Damien's brother and his two friends. Mike lifts his bag and sits beside me. He pulls out two sandwiches, and hands me one.

'Thanks,' I say.

'No worries.'

'Yo?'

'Yo.'

'We rocked 'em, didn't we?' I ask.

Mike takes a bite of his sandwich. He grins. 'Yeah, we did!'

Cathy Smith
from *Shifting Sands,* a novel

Chapter 1. Kuwait. The Desert

They had come ten miles from Kuwait City to the desert, along the three lane highway that ran in a straight line all the way from Saudi to Iraq. Giant pylons marched across the sand into the distance. Posters saying 'God bless the USA' or 'Thank God for America' flapped from telegraph poles. Bethan had wanted to drive to prove herself the capable woman but when they turned off the road heading into the dunes, without a landmark in sight, she was glad Steve was the driver. Undulating sand stretched for miles, exactly the same in every direction. At a point unmarked by any road-sign, Steve turned right. Two wolf-like dogs came out of nowhere and chased the jeep, barking and yelping. The noise echoed off the vehicle, exaggerating the isolation. Deep, blurred at the edge, paw-prints marked the trail of the dogs as they gave chase. Beside her, Bethan felt Steve trembling.

'Good job we don't need to get out.' His voice shook. 'Those babies would have your leg off as soon as look at you.' He was the first manager she'd employed when setting up her company eight years before, enticing him away from the security of the large company they had both worked for since the early eighties. Since then, they'd erected camps to feed and water the Forces or remote workers all over the world. She never boasted of their success but he did.

'Surely you're not scared of a couple of wild dogs, Steve?'

'Who, me? What do you think...?' Bethan wondered if he was trying to convince her or himself.

'You're the person we choose to sort the shit in difficult places. You always do it, too.' She pushed the dogs to the back of her mind and pursued this line of thought.

'Doesn't it get you down, even sometimes, all this danger and discomfort?'

She was curious about him, the boyish cheek that belied his forty years and made him irresistible to most women. His very blue eyes caressed every female he looked at. His nostrils crinkled sexily every time he breathed. He smelt of carbolic soap, fresh and clean. Both remembered the boozy night when his seduction had all but succeeded with her. Though tempted, she'd gone to bed alone, and then lain awake for hours, her reputation intact but her thoughts frenzied. It didn't seem to bother him that sex would get in the way of their relationship and it certainly wouldn't harm his reputation. It did not seem fair.

'No, don't be bloody stupid. Why would I be scared of a couple of old dogs?' His cockney accent became more evident.

The barking receded into the distance, replaced by a soft shrieking that built in intensity, drowning out the whir of the engine. Now the air tasted of dry dust. Both rubbed their eyes, laughing at the simultaneity of their actions.

'Shit, look at that.' With a slight jerk of his head, Steve indicated ahead. In the distance, coming towards them fast was a black swirl of whipped-up sand, tornado-like. It spread out along the horizon, changing its shape to long and thin. Bringing the jeep to a sharp halt, Steve craned his neck and scanned the way they had come.

'What you looking for?' She breathed faster and heard her tone sharpen.

'I just need to know where those bloody dogs have gone, before we get engulfed by this sodding sand-storm.'

'Bugger the dogs.' She shouted to be heard above the howl of the storm. 'It's this weather that'll get us.'

'We'll be fine if we just stay put. The jeep is strong enough to withstand the blast so we just need to wait till it passes.' Calm now, Steve had taken charge.

The sky blackened and large grains of sand blasted against the windscreen. A layer of fine sand stuck to the glass, and the wipers lost the battle to clear the window. Bethan tried to get out of the jeep, the gale catching the door and wrenching it from her hand. In seconds, the shrill wind and dust whipped her eyelids, forcing her back inside to her seat. Drawing her right leg across her left knee, she flicked sand off the designer trainers she had bought in her favourite shop in Verona. It settled in the crease of the black mat, making a narrow beach under her feet. She closed her eyes and shivered.

'Are you bloody mental? I told you to stay put. What possessed you?' Steve was shouting, so she opened her eyes and saw the tension in the muscles on his face. The collar of his crisp cotton shirt, standing up at the back of his neck, rustled when he turned his head. Its blueness reflected the brightness of his eyes. Two vertical tracks, each an inch long, appeared between his eyebrows as he frowned, and the laughter lines around his eyes tautened. Resisting the impulse to smooth his cheek, she sat on her hands and looked down at her shoes, 'I like risk, as long as men aren't involved...'

The noise increased. The sky became darker until it was impossible to see more than a few feet in front of them through the gritty fog. The jeep swayed, jerked by the wind, and Steve hummed softly, monotone, in time to the sand drumming on the glass. To abate her panic, she glanced sideways at him. She would take her cue from him; if he was not afraid, neither was she.

'Are your parents alive?' His question came out of the blue. Was he trying to distract her from her fear?

'My dad died about ten years ago, still miss him like hell. My mum's still alive. Does fantastically, although she's well into her eighties. How about you?' She raised her voice to compete with the grind of sand on the jeep.

'My dad is dead. Long dead. I'm glad. Deserved everything that came to him.' He stopped abruptly and stared out of the side window, yet could not see through the gloom. The small, fluffy camel hanging from the central mirror swung back and forth, creaking.

'He was a safe-breaker, you know. Worked for the Kray brothers. Spent most of his time inside, and when out, spent all his time beating up my mother. When I was sixteen, I was bigger and fitter than him.'

'Shit, must have been tough. Is your mother still alive?'

'No, she died last year. She was happy after he died,' he added and sort of smiled but his eyes stayed steely. She asked when his father had died and he replied, 'Not long after I was sixteen.'

In the silence that followed, the sand-storm eased, passed the jeep and continued back the way they had come. Daylight replaced the dismal air. 'Look, it's going. Good plan.' Steve cleared his throat. 'Stop me talking any more shit about my family. Sorry to impose it on you. Must have been the storm that got me thinking about him. Let's go.'

Before he could turn the key in the ignition, two eyes stared in and the mouth, snarling and baring teeth, filled the windscreen. As the dog pressed its face against the glass, Bethan gasped, watching its eyes, black and intelligent, fixed on Steve. Its mouth gaped, revealing stained teeth with razor-sharp ends. Mangy fur obliterated the view of the becalmed sand. The second dog scratched the side of the van, growling and loud.

Steve started the engine, put his foot flat to the floor and watched the dog try to make its paws stick to the metallic surface. It failed and slid off the side of the bonnet, bouncing on the tail bar before it was thrown onto the sand. Trying to stand, it raised itself half on its legs and staggered on the spot. Steve whirled the jeep around a full 180 degrees and accelerated towards it. Bethan watched with her hand over her mouth as mangled limbs and fur were flung into the air. As in slow motion, the beast hung before it fell to the ground, breaking through the shimmer that hovered over the sand. It lay motionless.

'He had a dog, my father,' Steve smiled wryly. 'My dad had a bloody dog.'

Back in her hotel room in the city, Bethan perched on her bed hugging her legs before climbing into the oversized bath tub, luxuriant with white spice gel, to rid her body and hair of the clinging sand. Although she tried to focus her mind on where to get bottled water for the Americans, she drifted into a replay of the day. She closed her eyes and breathed deeply, before immersing herself, the scent and softness caressing her skin. Sitting up, spilling bathwater and bubbles onto the marble tiled floor, she ran her fingers through her hair to push it back from her forehead. Drops of water ran down both sides of her face. The phone ringing dragged her from her daydream. She reached for it with a soapy hand.

'Hello, Bethan Sands,' she said, thankful this was not a video phone.

'Bettanee, I need to talk to you.'

'Ali, hi. How are you? What's the problem?'

'You must come and see me tomorrow. I must talk to you, it's important, Bettanee. You can bring Steve.' She hated the way he pronounced her name, trying to be so Arabic, disguising his Eton accent.

'What's so urgent?' She spoke to a dialling tone. He had gone.

Cathy Smith
Gloves

She stood back from the border and clapped her hands to shake loose the drying mud from her gardening gloves. Soothed by the muffled thudding, she cupped her palms and clapped faster. Her whole body shuddered when she caught sight of a tear in the top of the thumb and glimpsed a flash of white skin beneath. Forcing her gaze away from the glove to the long display of red and white flowers, she willed the panic to stop before it started.

'Red geraniums grow best, red geraniums grow best.' She mouthed the words, talking her shoulders down to rid the tension from the back of her neck while trying to think of something else. In one of the newspapers that she pored over every day she had read that championship-winning sports teams wear red more than any colour. She liked red. The bedraggled borders that edged the tarmac road between the big black iron gates and the security lodge had been transformed by her two lines of scarlet geraniums and busy-lizzies, interspersed with the white lobelia. No expense was to be spared for the forthcoming royal tour but there were limits. As instructed, she had hidden the pots under the soil so that they could be dug up and sent back to the nursery when the Queen's visit was over.

Glancing up at the rectangular concrete building, she wondered again how creative architects could have been happy with the two lines of small windows, their vertical metal bars obscuring the view of anyone trying to look out. With the compost bag full of weeds and her trowel in her hands, she walked back towards the lodge. The sky greyed as it began to drizzle, so she broke into a run to escape the rain.

'Jennings, are you going back in now?' the officer at the gatehouse barked, adding in a softer tone, 'You've made a stunning job of that. Didn't know we had a budding gardener in our midst.' He laughed at his own joke but she did not smile.

'You had better leave those things here,' he said. 'Just put them in the corner and I'll put them away later.' She put down the trowel and dropped the bag alongside. It fell on its side. Straggly weeds and small stones spilled across the red quarry tiles. The officer ignored the mishap. Boredom was carved deep in his face as he turned back to his computer, to resume his mindless input of data.

She found the common room empty. As a trusty she was allowed to spend time there but it was depressing. The room was large and draughty, painted in that yellowy cream that must have been bought, she thought, as a job lot. Greying notices, overlapping each other, were fastened to the wall with curling sellotape. Topics ranged from fire evacuation procedures to the library rules, from courses of creative study to newspaper articles on prison reforms. The only one ever read was the distinctive green poster of the Samaritans.

At the back of the room, three tiny booths played host to three old and oversized computers. As she walked towards them, she heard a snigger behind her.

'Bloody 'ell, Jenks. You on them fucking computers again? Thought you were tarting up our gardens for the bloody queen.'

Turning around, she saw Collins and smiled, a smile that changed to a grimace when Parkes walked in behind.

'Don't fuck about with her, Col. She's just a fuckin' goody two-shoes, creeping up the gov'nor's ass.' Her cigarette end glowed intensely for a second as she took a deep puff.

'Red ends glow best, red ends glow best, red ends glow best.' Had she said these words aloud or in her head? As quickly as they had arrived and for no apparent reason, the two women turned and left, leaving a swirl of grey smoke curling up into the air. Running into the nearside booth, she almost threw herself down on the stool in front of the computer desk, opened the top drawer and pulled out a pair of white cotton gloves.

She closed her eyes tightly as she ripped off the muddy gardening gloves and replaced them with these pristine finger-hugging sheaths, straining to pull them on. She sucked in air in quick gasps, and her face puckered as she wrestled them onto her hands. Only when they were both in place did she open her eyes to check. Sitting perfectly still on the stool, she breathed slowly in and out, until her body shrugged off its tension.

When she pressed the 'on' switch, the screen-saver picture of herself at the helm of a fire engine made her relax. Strangely, nobody had objected to her personalising the computer in a world where items were fiercely protected and often fought over. She did not really need any mark of identity—most of the inmates felt, anyway, that the computer was hers. With her eyes fixed on the screen she tapped the keys quickly and competently.

'Twenty-three years of study and a wicked brain,' she thought to herself. 'I must be the only forty-year-old in the country with three degrees and no chance to do any good with any of 'em.' She laughed. 'Well, maybe I'm kidding myself. I'm too timid to be any use outside even if I did have the chance.'

In her head, the words started, 'Red engines fight fires best, red engines fight fires best.' She rubbed her gloved hands through her hair, blonde and cut short in a layered bob.

The boys at the fire station had told her she looked like a tomboy, but a cute one, and Dave, the young trainee had added cheekily, 'Yeah, and sexy too.' Uncertain whether it was right to feel good about that, she had not replied, but inside had experienced a new feeling; she had found an okay place to be.

In the computer screen she caught a reflection of the gloves. A momentary flash of whiteness seemed to burn her brain and she closed her eyes to block it out. Opening them again, she peeled back her left sleeve, exposing the red scars, faded a bit but clearly visible even after twenty odd years. The smell of burning skin, from cigarette-ends pressed into her small body, still lingered in the back of her throat. She had learned early to stop screaming, a small victory over the stepmother who delighted in her cries of agony. Instead, she had followed the patterns as they formed in the redness on her skin, imagining jewels on her forearms, and the pain had lessened.

'Red rubies hurt less, red rubies hurt less.' She had chanted these words every day for twelve years, like a mantra, as she had rocked on her haunches, trying to hide in the floor in the corner of her small room. It was not a good hiding place. Like many children she believed herself to be invisible when she closed her eyes, out of sight of her parents. Day after day she screwed her eyes tightly shut and made no noise, praying silently that she would be ignored. More often than not, this approach failed and she was dragged from her corner retreat to join the adult world. She never knew why she was battered. She tried so hard to be a good girl. The day that her world exploded, when the hatred burst out of her, was still a blank in her memory. But she could clearly see the glint of the knife and feel the stickiness of the blood on her hands.

'Red blood flows best, red blood flows best.' She did not stop saying this as they took her to the police station, as they left her in the corner of the cell, once more rocking on her haunches, once more trying to hide.

'Jennings, you have a visitor.' The officer's voice dragged her back to the present. 'It's the guy from the Fire Brigade and he's in the Governor's office. You're to go and see them. They're waiting for you.'

Mr Andrews, the Chief Fire Officer, was seated across the desk from the Governor. His dark blue uniform was well-pressed, and she liked the way he'd put his cap squarely on the edge of the desk, as if waiting for an inspection of its own.

'Come in, Jennings, have a seat.' The Governor's voice was kindly but her shoulders tensed. 'Mr Andrews wants to have a chat with you. Don't worry, it's good news.'

'Good news?' Her voice was shaky. On the desk, a wooden bowl of fruit attracted her attention, purple plums leaning against the tickly greenish skins of the kiwis, orange clementines standing out against the bright yellow bananas. In her head she started repeating 'red apples taste best, red apples taste best' and hoped these words were silent.

'Sally,' he said. 'You have been coming to us for work experience for over two years now. You've made great progress with our IT systems. We have been very pleased with all of your efforts.'

Oh no, she thought. They're going to sack me and then I will have nowhere to go where I belong. Red apples taste best, red apples taste best. Her gloved fingers scratched out the rhythm of the words on her overalls, cotton on cotton. She put her hands under her thighs and sat on them so that they were stilled and out of sight.

'There is a vacancy in our central office in Gloucester for someone to help with the route planning of the fire engines. We need a new computer system and we could use your talents.' She looked across at him, realisation dawning. 'We can recommend you for it.'

'Is it possible? Do they really want me in a proper job? Can I go?' She addressed this last question to the Governor.

'Jennings, your time here is nearly up. This is an open prison so you can go to work as part of your rehabilitation. Eventually you'll move to a hostel.' The Governor was monotone in his explanation. 'Having a job is a big step forward.'

Sally Jennings hung on his every word, ignoring the flatness of voice. She leant forward and willed her memory to assimilate all the details until the conversation finished. She did not know how to react to good news, how to overturn years of holding emotion in check. She hoped that she could learn.

When she got back to the cell, Collins was sitting on her bed.

'Bloody 'ell, Col! I've got a job. I've got a bloody job!' Her voice was shrill.

'What do you mean? What job?' Collins was incredulous.

'You know, Col. At the fire station, in the computer department, where I am now, you know!' The words tripped each other up. 'They want me to help to plan new routes for the fire engines!' She was trying to regain her breath.

She stared at the white cotton gloves and her face paled to much the same colour. She had told the guys at the station that she wore gloves because she had dermatitis and needed to cover her hands. It was a lie, and she knew that they knew it was a lie. Slumping down on her bed she turned her face to the wall and Collins understood she would say no more.

Hours later, while it was still just light, she stood and held the gloved hands up in front of her, level with her face.

'I can beat this, I can beat this, I can beat this.' She kept her eyes open this time as she slowly and deliberately peeled the gloves from her trembling fingers, and for the first time in twenty-three years, studied her own hands.

Cathy Smith

An Ayrshire Cemetery

The North Sea's gales howl through the headstones,
row after row of uniform grey granite.
My favourite uncle, killed at his work,
in the row reserved for all those dead on that day.
My grandparents close, and I feel their closeness.
My baby cousin, claimed by TB—
no flowers now his mother shares his space.
His sister, father, cousins; Kings and Patersons.
Thirteen family plots, a Scottish clan, together, family-minded.
I feel the sense of belonging, here in death,
I used to long for from my distant English life.

John Whittles
Medicine

The stitch was getting worse.

His right hand was in his jacket pocket and in his hand were the last three ampoules. The glass was delicate. He held them gently. Holding them reminded him why he was running. It also stopped them from breaking against each other. That had happened before and he didn't want to go back again tonight. He slowed to a walk as he emerged onto Jackson. He sniffed and spat and stared at his trainers avoiding cracks. His car was only three blocks away. He gently rolled the ampoules around in his hand like they were Baoding balls. It was getting harder to walk but the distant sirens made him want to keep going until he got to the car. He breathed deep and thought about tonight. He'd never had to smash a window to get out before. The new guard was quicker than the others. Heavier. He snorted and spat. He could see his car.

He was two blocks away but the pain was bad enough to make him stop at the next lamppost. He kept his hand around the ampoules and rested his shoulder on the metal and let it hold his weight. He closed his eyes and looked up at the sky. Then he opened his eyes wide. Beyond the orange glare he could see a clear night. The moon was bright and three quarters full. He breathed deep but still the stitch ate his side. He looked down and saw something he hadn't seen before. There was a tear in his jacket. Just above the left pocket and about the length of a cigarette packet. He traced the line with his finger. The fabric around it was dark and damp. His finger entered the hole. Then it found something sharp. The stitch screamed and he let go of the ampoules in his pocket. His left leg buckled and he fell to a crouch. He gripped the lamppost.

He let out a whine and let go of the metal. Then he got up and checked the ampoules and started walking towards his car. He knew he shouldn't have stopped. The pain in his side was worse now and he noticed he was limping. He sniffed and swallowed. He unzipped his jacket as he walked. When the zipper was half way down he looked inside. The bottom of his t-shirt was shiny and wet and something under the tear in his jacket glinted in the moonlight. He zipped up the zipper and walked a little faster. He started rolling the ampoules around in his hand again. Then he crossed the street.

    Daniel tried not to think of the blood he was losing. The blood he had lost. He listened to the night. All he could hear was the sound of his trainers dragging on the sidewalk. He thought about the clinic. Daniel remembered when Frank was on the gate. He would let you have whatever you needed as long as you showed him some respect and a twenty. Frank just wanted a quiet night. He was a good guy. The clinic didn't agree. Daniel had felt responsible when they got rid of Frank but he figured that he wasn't the only person Frank was helping out. When Daniel got to his car he reached in his jeans and pulled the keys out and put them in the door. Then he flicked some blood from his hand. He couldn't remember when he got hurt but he had to figure his injury was pretty serious. He unlocked the door and opened it and sat down quickly. Pain swarmed from his side all around his leg and across his stomach and his chest. He gripped the steering wheel with both hands. A minute later he let go of the wheel and shut the door.

    He looked in the rear view mirror. It might have just been the moonlight but he thought he looked pretty pale. With his right hand he carefully pulled down the zipper on his jacket. He pulled the jacket apart and rolled his right shoulder back and slipped his arm out. Then he unwrapped the jacket from around his other arm. He let the jacket fall behind the seat and looked down. He saw that his shirt was wetter and stickier than before. The blood seemed to be coming from a tear in his t-shirt that was identical to the one in his jacket. He peeled up his t-shirt. Daniel saw that the tear went all the way through to his skin. Just under his ribcage there was a dark slash oozing blood. He could see two small triangles of glass poking out from either end of the wound. They pointed away from each other and were coated in blood. He pulled his t-shirt back down and started the car. A black and white cat ran out from underneath a hedge and bolted across the road without stopping. Daniel watched it as it disappeared behind a parked car on the other side of the street. Then he rolled the window down and snorted and spat as he pulled away.

    He stopped at the first liquor store he saw. Before he got out of the car he thought about putting his jacket back on but he didn't want to have to take it off again so he just got out of the car. He had to use the door to pull himself out. He felt drunk. When he was on his feet he reached in and got his jacket from behind the seat. He held it against his side and limped into the store. The guy behind the counter looked at him real funny but still sold him a bottle of Four Roses and two fake Roadrunner t-shirts. When he got back in his car he tossed everything on the passenger seat and drove a little down the street and parked in an alley. He flipped the light in the car and flipped it off again. Then he took off his t-shirt and looked at himself in the mirror. He thought he was definitely looking pretty pale. His chest looked like the skin on frozen chicken thighs. He grabbed the whiskey, opened it and took a large swig into his mouth. Then he moved the bottle and poured half of it down his side. He swallowed and pushed his head back into the headrest. Then he put the bottle between his legs and grabbed one of the new t-shirts from the passenger seat. He bit into the thin plastic around it and unwrapped it.

He wiped the whiskey-blood from his stomach and patted down the wound and looked at it. He knew what he had to do but he didn't want to do it here. Then he remembered the medicine. He hadn't seen it since he got into his car on Jackson Street. Panic swept away his pain. He kept Roadrunner on his side with his left hand and with his right he rummaged in his jacket on the passenger seat. He reached in the pocket. Empty. He fumbled for the next one. Empty. His eyes darted in between the seats. Nothing. He felt behind his seat. He felt broken glass. The pain in his side got worse. The floor around the glass was dry which meant the liquid inside had already evaporated. He snorted. He moved his fingers around some more. He felt something roll away from them. Then he found one. And another. He picked the ampoules up and sat back and clutched them to his chest. He put them in the glove box and drank some more whiskey. Then he put the bottle between his legs and drove away.

He pulled into his street an hour and twenty minutes later. It was a quarter after four in the morning. The first Roadrunner shirt was saturated and crumpled next to the empty bottle on the passenger seat. He had had to apply the second shirt while driving about a half hour before. He was holding it to his side with his left hand and could feel that it was already pretty damp. He turned into the drive and parked his Honda next to a green SUV. He killed the engine. The house was dark. He sniffed. Then he checked the glove box. The medicine was safe. He flicked on the light and looked at his face in the mirror. He shut off the light and opened the car door. He had had the heat full on in the car and the cold air stung his chest. He picked up his jacket and wrapped it around his bare shoulders. He pulled the medicine from the glove box and flipped it shut. He put the ampoules on the dashboard and used the door to pull himself out of the car. Then he reached back in and grabbed the medicine and shut the door with his foot. He put the medicine in his jacket pocket. He shuffled to the front door and hit his head on one of the hanging baskets. He had left all his keys in the ignition but the door was unlocked so he opened it and went inside.

The hallway was silent except for the breathing of the machine in the next room. Through the open door ahead of him he could see the outline of his wife on the sofa. She was asleep and covered with a blanket. He stopped to kick his shoes off. An old Alsatian dog came in from the kitchen and nuzzled the back of his legs. He lay at Daniel's feet and covered his grey nose in his paws and looked up at him. When Daniel turned around he looked at the dog and the dog whined quietly. Daniel shuffled down the hall and the dog got up and followed him. He stopped in the open doorway and watched his wife for a moment. Then he closed the door in front of him. He shuffled round the hall and stopped at the door to the next room. He opened the door and walked inside. The dog came in after Daniel and Daniel shut the door behind them. He turned on the desk lamp and the dog walked over to the machine and lay down in front of it.

Daniel walked over and touched the viewing window and looked at his son. Valves hissed and clicked as the machine inhaled and exhaled for the boy. Daniel didn't know how he slept with the noise. He took his hand away and saw he had left bloody fingerprints on the glass. He used the arm of his jacket to wipe them away. Daniel sniffed and moved to the side of the machine and started twisting a small brass wheel that was on top of one of the pipes. The wheel clicked and he pulled it up. From under the wheel came a metal cylinder with six chambers. It was like the cylinder of a revolver except it loaded from the side not the top.

He reached inside the pocket and pulled out the two glass ampoules. He slid each ampoule into a separate chamber and pushed the cylinder back down and turned the wheel. He moved back to the window and pushed a button on the side of the machine. The loading mechanism whirred inside the pipe and he heard the glass crack. He looked at his son and smiled and closed his eyes. Then he moved across the room and sat at his desk.

Daniel reached in the top drawer and pulled out a quarter-empty bottle of Four Roses and drank from it. He put the bottle on the desk and stared at the machine. Daniel knew it would outlive the boy. Not that the machine was alive. Or that the boy had ever really lived. Daniel picked up the bottle and drank some more. Daniel remembered the first time they put the boy in the machine. It was two weeks before his third birthday and the first time they were able to bring him home. He was in the local paper. He had been in the hospital since he was born. Daniel remembered being so full of hope then. Later that same month the clinic heard about the boy and announced they were including him in an experimental trial. The medicine they gave him was incredible. After the first dose the boy started breathing on his own. He still had to sleep in the machine but in the day he could get out and walk around. He could go outside. They played catch. The medicine was so good they stopped the trial early. Turned out this medicine could be used for all types of lung problems. That meant they could charge top dollar for it. And top dollar was too expensive for Daniel and his wife. They had re-mortgaged the house to buy the machine and no insurance company would touch the boy at a rate they could afford. Without the medicine Daniel watched his son wilt. His lungs just dried up and he became more and more dependent on the machine. Daniel went to the papers but they weren't interested this time. Then Daniel found out where they manufactured the medicine.

He let go of the Roadrunner shirt and put it on his desk. He moved the lamp toward him. He drank some more whiskey and then he poured some down his side. He sniffed. He put the bottle on the desk and with his right thumb and forefinger pinched one of the glass triangles. He counted to three in his head and pulled. The piece came out smoothly but it was bigger than he thought it would be. He heard blood dapple the carpet. He thought about his life insurance policy. In his fingers Daniel held a crescent-shaped shard of glass. He thought it looked like a quarter moon. He held it in front of the lamp to get a better look. The glass slipped from his fingers and fell on to the desk. The light was too bright so he closed his eyes and felt around in front of him and knocked the Four Roses onto the floor. Then he found the piece of glass. He gripped it in his hand and laid his arm on the desk and rested his forehead on his arm and went to sleep. Then the dog got up and walked over and sat at his feet.

Nia Wyn
Trauma and the Creative Process

This essay explores the relationship between trauma[1] and creativity and examines in particular the process of recovery from trauma through writing. It will be considered in both a personal context, with reference to my memoir *Blue Sky July*,[2] and in a wider and more literary context.

In his book, *Lessons from a Lifetime of Writing*, David Morrell argues that writers write because they have to and that writers who discover what sets them apart have the best chance of succeeding.[3] He refers to fiction-writing as self-psychoanalysis and says:

> Most people become writers because they're haunted by secrets they need to tell. The writers might not know they have secrets, or if they suspect they do, they might not be sure what these mysteries are, but something in each person is bursting to get out, to be revealed.[4]

According to Morrell, any psychological trauma never adjusted to can be the impetus for someone wanting to be a storyteller.[5]

Of course not all creativity springs out of trauma, but there is a significant amount of literature that suggests a strong correlation between traumatic events in authors' lives and the writing they produce. Prisons, oppressed children and the suffering of the poor are constant themes in the work of Charles Dickens who was forced to be a labourer in a squalid factory when his father was imprisoned for debts.[6] Many characters in the plays of Tennessee Williams are also regarded as having their origins in his own troubled upbringing; for example one might consider Laura Wingfield in *The Glass Menagerie* to have been inspired by his sister Rose who suffered from schizophrenia.[7] We might also look at Raskolnikov's dream of a mare being beaten in Dostoyevsky's *Crime and Punishment* in this context.[8] According to Gilbert Rose, it is the author's way of mastering his own childhood trauma of seeing a horse being beaten to death in his youth.[9] Hemingway certainly understood the importance of trauma to a writer. In a letter to F. Scott Fitzgerald in 1934, he advised, 'We are all bitched from the start and you especially have to be hurt like hell before you can write seriously.'[10]

The relationship between trauma and writing is especially interesting to me as, although I cannot claim to have produced art from trauma in the literary sense referred to above, I have been able to experience a deepening in terms of my own creative process in this regard. While I wrote poems and short stories as a child and subsequently enjoyed a 15-year spell as an award-winning journalist and feature writer, it is only since a recent trauma in my life that I have begun to experience a relationship with writing as something that I have to—rather than to choose to—do.

I had fully expected to have a life-changing experience in the summer of 1998 when I left my work as a feature writer to have a much-wanted baby. What I had not expected, however, was that it would be so in the sense it proved to be. Not only did I become a mother that summer, but I became a mother to a child who, due to a trauma at birth, was left with the most severe form of disability—cerebral palsy. As a consequence of this, the charmed and happy relationship I had previously enjoyed with life was suddenly turned upside down and I was cast into a vortex of confusion and despair which for me, as I was to write sometime later in my memoir *Blue Sky July*, was like, 'a total eclipse'.[11]

To examine this period of my life within a critical study of the relationship between trauma and creativity is particularly appropriate because if, as many writers believe, the demands of young children interfere with the undistracted time and intellectual freedom considered necessary to produce substantial creative work, my ability to write should have been interrupted to a higher degree, and for a longer period, than most. On top of the general requirements of parenthood, such was my son's disability that I became his arms, his legs, his eyes, his voice; and any scraps of free time were filled with the most relentless therapy routines and emotional trauma of the deepest kind. It was, however, during this period in my life (while also battling the common symptoms associated with trauma, such as insomnia, listlessness and an inability to concentrate) that I produced a book that was my most substantial and artistic work to date.

So what, I must ask myself, compelled me to write at this time more seriously than I ever had before? And what were the ingredients of this irresistible force that drove it through the seemingly immovable object consisting of all these odds stacked up against it on the other side?

It would be possible to draw comparisons between my feelings of marginalization, separation, isolation and misery that resulted from this traumatic event in my life, with those experienced by other writers who also felt compelled to express them in their work. Virginia Woolf, for example, proposes the creation of an 'Outsiders' Society' in her strongly feminist work *Three Guineas*[12] and D H Lawrence, the son of a coal miner, also identified with the role, describing his unhappy childhood home in his autobiographical novel *Sons and Lovers*.[13] The American poet Anne Sexton, who won the Pulitzer prize for poetry in 1967, found the impetus to write in the depths of despair and, like Robert Lowell, W.D Snodgrass and other confessional poets, offers the reader an intimate view of the emotional anguish that characterized her life. Sylvia Plath, another Pulitzer prize-winning poet, was also trapped in the feelings of isolation and misery when at her most prolific. In her only novel *The Belljar*, the main protagonist's descent into mental illness is widely considered to reflect Plath's own experiences with clinical depression.[14]

That trauma can provide an impetus to write cannot be denied. However, although I acknowledge that such feelings of despair created my own need to write at this time, during the writing process I experienced a gradual shift away from this traumatized state which also suggests to me that a relationship between writing and the healing of trauma might be equally valid.

According to research psychologist James Pennebaker, the simple act of writing can have a profound effect on the health of those suffering a trauma. In his book *Writing To Heal, A Guided Journal for Recovering from Trauma and Emotional Upheaval*, he refers to scientific studies that have found writing to be a tool for healing and lists the medical and physical benefits that are proven to result from it.[15] Emotional upheavals touch every area of our lives, Pennebaker explains:

> You don't just lose a job, you don't just get divorced. These things affect all aspects of who we are—our financial situation, our relationships with others, our view of ourselves, our issues of life and death. Writing helps us focus and organize the experience.[16]

Pennebaker says that when a traumatic event occurs, our minds have to work overtime to process the experience and that writing can make it more manageable: 'People who are able to construct a story, to build some kind of narrative over the course of their writing seem to benefit more than those who don't.'[17]

This is a view shared by Daniel Goleman in his book *Emotional Intelligence*, in which he advocates the articulation of traumatic experience as a pivotal factor in the healing process:

> By putting sensory details and feeling into words, presumably memories are brought more under the control of the neocortex, where the reactions they kindle can be rendered more understandable and so more manageable.[18]

Goleman's book also suggests that even the most deeply implanted habits can be reshaped and that emotional learning is lifelong.[19]

When reflecting on my own creative process, it is possible for me to identify key elements that I believe had a cathartic effect at different times and in different ways. Following an initial period of simply expressing my thoughts and feelings on paper in the dead of night, a period accompanied by anguish and bouts of sobbing, I entered a more meditative relationship with my subject matter and began to search for meaning in this heartbreak. I was still, at this stage, not so much interested in the artistic merit of the writing as I was in finding a meaning and a purpose that would lead me out of my despair and help me transcend it. Writing at this time felt more like a meditation or a prayer, and the act of sitting at my lap-top like an act of survival.

Things began to happen almost mysteriously on the page during this period and, in creative terms, I felt inspired. It was as if I was being led by something either within or outside me that helped me draw new connections and patterns out of the flood of writing on the page. When I wrote the words began to feel more lyrical as if I'd tapped into a deeper music, and a more poetic style emerged. During the periods away from my lap-top, it seemed as if my ordinary, everyday routines and moments also took on new associations in my mind which fed into the writing and I experienced occasional periods of an almost exalted mood in the discovery of new perspectives.

Although I do not subscribe to any religion, it is perhaps

important to mention here that having studied theology for my honours degree, I certainly reflected upon and felt inspired by spiritual concepts as my writing developed and there is, indeed, a religious context for the kind of creative process I experienced in this light. The phrase 'Dark Night of the Soul' (the title of a sixteenth- century mystical text written by the Carmelite monk St. John of the Cross) is popularly used today to describe a period of loneliness and desolation in one's life which makes room for a change that can bring about transformation. In the Bible, Paul of Tarsus describes God's strength as being most evident in his own weakness[20] and Jacob saw God in the night in the fight that crippled him.[21] The implication here is that God works with us when we suffer. When I refer to this stage of my writing as feeling inspired and mysterious, it is important to me to at least acknowledge such texts as I felt supported and strengthened in my conviction to write at this time which gave the writing itself a new depth and tension.

In *Man's Search for Meaning*, the Austrian neurologist and psychiatrist Viktor Frankl points out that when we are able to give our traumas meaning, a healing can begin to take place.[22] In his moving account of his imprisonment in Auschwitz and his struggle during this time to find reasons to live, Frankl says that, when trying to cure fellow prisoners of their despondency and prevent suicide, he identified an ability to give meaning to the struggle as a key factor in those prisoners who were able to survive it: 'What matters, therefore, is not the meaning of life in general, but rather the specific meaning of a person's life at a given moment.'[23] According to Frankl we discover this meaning in life in three different ways: '(1) by creating a work or doing a deed; (2) by experiencing something or encountering someone; and (3) by the attitude we take towards unavoidable suffering.'[24] Interestingly for Frankl, himself, who had had a manuscript confiscated when taken to Auschwitz, it was in the desire to write that he found meaning: '…my deep desire to write this manuscript anew helped me to survive the rigours of the camps I was in.'[25]

When I began to look for meaning in my own personal struggle, it was also through writing that I was mysteriously able to find, if not the answers, then at least valuable insights which helped me consider my situation in different ways. I now began to see what seemed to be the true story emerge and started piecing it together into a cohesive whole. At this stage the work developed a style of short, broken-up passages of text and I introduced its themes of dark and light. This editing phase was focused and rapid. It was as if by some innate, though also (following my years in journalism) some professional instinct perhaps, I simply knew what I was doing. In retrospect, it is also apparent that by being able to work in this way again, a healing of some kind had taken place and I felt fully in control of what I wanted the words to say.

Gilbert Rose refers to the transforming quality of creativity in his book *Trauma and Mastery in Life and Art* and believes art, like psychoanalysis, awakens one to submerged and split-off currents of feeling: As a result of the interplay of imagination and knowledge, the artwork strikes a new balance between internal and external. What began as the common task of mastering one's personal past, becomes for the creative artist a process of externalizing and transcending it—to disclose new aspects of reality itself.'[26]

According to Rose, art like psychoanalysis draws, 'on the wellsprings of feeling, via aesthetic form and memory, helping to reintegrate it with thought and perception [...].This is a form of inner mastery which is conducive to growth.'[27]

It is, however, with reference to the fourth and final stage of my creative process that I'm able to offer a deeper perspective on the complex nature of the relationship that exists between trauma and writing. On completion of my memoir, I had such a strong sense that the act of writing itself had transported me from a place of extreme suffering to a place where I felt that I could cope again, that I decided to send off this intensely personal account of my life with my son for publication, in the hope that it might also help others in similar situations. The success this book has had and the huge response there has been to it has surprised me, and has led me to wonder what secret lies within its pages that has connected so deeply with so many in this way.

William Anderson, in his book *Dante the Maker*, says that works of art are storehouses of psychic energy and transmit this energy according to the quality of attention the reader brings to them.[28] Among the effects of this energy, he says, is a willing surrender of our private concerns to a universal experience: There is a certain point on coming into contact with a work of art when one seems suddenly to connect with its emotional or symbolic message. Unless there is this connection which rivets attention on the work it makes no more than a shallow impression.[29]

Anderson goes on to describe a further stage 'in which the barriers separating the inner life of the enjoyer and the essence of the work of art seem to dissolve, and the enjoyer is conscious of being united with the particular mood and insight out of which the work was created.'[30] This is the state, he believes, described by T.S. Eliot, 'as music heard so deeply/That it is not heard at all, but you are the music/While the music lasts.'[31] The reader, says Anderson, can only experience this deep unifying awareness if the artist has achieved a similar union between his subject and his execution of it in the way that Dante described in his *canzone* on nobility: 'For he who paints a face/Cannot succeed unless he is it first.'[32]

Certainly for me it has been the readers' response to my memoir, (especially in terms of the deeply personal and heart-felt letters that I have received) that has been the most rewarding stage in this creative process. Many readers have said that the book has been an emotional journey for them too, and has helped them work through their own private agonies. This makes me realize that my own cathartic experience of writing trauma has in some way transcended my own relationship to this work and proved cathartic for others.

It is important to me to recognize the inspirational effect that working through one's own personal trauma in this way can have on others as it seems to be the message at the core of some of the earliest texts on the subject. In the Greek myth of Chiron, creativity is the supreme skill that allows the centaur, destined for a life of suffering following an accidental wound, to become the great healer.[33] Due to its themes of union, reconciliation and bridge-building, the myth is believed to have inspired Carl Gustav Jung's wounded healer archetype who transcends suffering and pain when he dedicates himself to the service of others.[34] In the final stage of my own creative process, I have started to give talks about the book to charities that help people in similar situations to my own as well as to those interested in working with children with special needs and, in this, I feel I have achieved a reintegration and unification with the world again.

Whilst trauma can be understood by some to be one of the

most critical and universal factors underpinning creativity (according to Hesoid's *Theogony*, creation sprang from a union between darkness and chaos[35]), the creative process each person undergoes as a result will be as individual as the trauma and work itself. Though many, like Alice Walker and Louise Salvo, believe that writing, 'can be a very sturdy ladder out of the pit,'[36] just a backward glance at some of the names mentioned at the start of this essay makes it clear that writing is not a cure-all. Hemingway, Woolf, Plath and Sexton all committed suicide and so it was, at best, a temporary means of coping with their suffering, if at all.

Perhaps the words of the poet Dannie Abse, who recently lost his wife in a car crash and tackles the subject in his highly personal memoir *The Presence*, are a suitable way to conclude. After reading excerpts in Waterstones on Hampstead High Street in September 2007, he said that trauma had at first made him extremely introverted and turned his thoughts to suicide, but that he declined therapy in favour of writing a journal. 'I don't think you ever get over bereavement,' he told the audience, 'but it's certainly helped me. I can and do count the alphabet of my blessings.'[37]

End Notes

1. Trauma, in this essay is used in the general, rather than strictly medical, sense, to refer to an emotional or psychological injury resulting from an extremely stressful situation.
2. Nia Wyn, *Blue Sky July* (Bridgend: Seren, 2007).
3. David Morrell, *Lessons from a lifetime of Writing: a novelist looks at his craft* (Cincinnati: Writer's Digest Books, 2002), pp.13-15.
4. Ibid., p.15.
5. Ibid., p.15.
6. Ibid., pp.15-16.
7. Tennessee Williams, *The Glass Menagerie* (London: Methuen Publishing Ltd, 2000).
8. Fyodor Dostoyevsky, *Crime and Punishment* (London: Penguin Classics, 2003), pp. 67-73.
9. Gilbert J Rose, *Trauma and Mastery in Life and Art* (New Haven and London: Yale University Press, 1923), pp. 29-35.
10. Ernest Hemingway, quoted in Marc Seals, 'Trauma Theory and Hemingway's Lost Paris Manuscripts', *Project MUSE: Scholarly Journals Online*. Available at http://muse.jhu.edu/login?uri=/journals/hemingway_review/v024/24.2seals.html [accessed 12 January 2008].
11. *Blue Sky July*, p. 24.
12. Virginia Woolf, *A Room of One's Own – Three Guineas* (Oxford: Oxford University Press, 1992) p. 309.
13. D. H. Lawrence, *Sons and Lovers*, (London: Penguin, 1995).
14. Sylvia Plath, *The Belljar*, (London: Faber and Faber, 1963).
15. James W. Pennebaker, *Writing To Heal, A Guided Journal for Recovering from Trauma and Emotional Upheaval* (Oakland: New Harbinger Publications Inc, 2004), pp. 7-10.
16. Pennebaker, quoted in Vive Griffith, 'Writing to Heal', *University of Texas website*: http://www.utexas.edu/features/2005/writing/ [accessed 10 January 2008).
17. Ibid.
18. Daniel Goleman, *Emotional Intelligence* (London: Bloomsbury, 1996), p. 212.
19. Ibid., p.214.
20. *The Bible,* 2 Corinthians 12
21. *The Bible,* Genesis 32
22. Viktor E. Frankl, *Man's Search for Meaning,* (New York: Pocket Books, 1985).
23. Ibid, p.131.
24. Ibid, p.133.

25. Ibid, p.126.
26. Rose, op. cit., p. 210.
27. Ibid, p. 215.
28. William Anderson, *Dante The Maker* (London: Routledge and Kegan Paul Ltd, 1980), p5.
29. Ibid, p.5.
30. Ibid, P.5.
31. T.S.Eliot, 'The Dry Salvages', *Four Quartets*, quoted in Anderson, p.5.
32. Dante, '*canzone* on nobility', quoted in Anderson, p.5.
33. Claire Dunne, *Carl Jung: Wounded Healer of the Soul* (Sandpoint: Morning Light Press 2000).
34. Robert Graves, The Greek Myths I, II, (London: The Folio Society Ltd, 1996).
35. Ibid., pp 41-42.
36. Alice Walker, quoted by Louise A Desalvo, *Writing As A Way of Healing: How Telling Our Stories Transforms Our Lives* (Boston: First Beacon Press, 2000), p.8.
37. Dannie Abse, quoted by Simon Wroe in *The Camden New Journal*, (Camden: New Journal Enterprises, October 2007). Available at h*ttp://www.thecnj.com/review/2007/100407/books100407_03.html* [accessed 11 January 2008).

Bibliography

Anderson, William, *Dante The Maker* (London: Routledge and Kegan Paul Ltd, 1980)

DeSalvo, Louise, A., *Writing As a Way of Healing: How Telling Our Stories Transforms Our Lives* (Boston:First Beacon Press, 2000)

Dostoyevsky, Fyodor, *Crime and Punishment* (London: Penguin Classics, 2003)

Dunne, Claire, *Carl Jung: Wounded Healer of the Soul* (Sandpoint: Morning Light Press, 2000)

Frankl, Viktor E., *Man's Search for Meaning* (New York: Pocket Books, 1985)

Goleman, Daniel, *Emotional Intelligence* (London: Bloomsbury, 1996)
Graves, Robert, *The Greek Myths I, II* (London: The Folio Society Ltd,

1996)

Griffith, Vive, Writing to Heal. *University of Texas website*. Available at http://www.utexas.edu/features/2005/writing/ [accessed 11 January, 2008]

Lawrence, D.H., *Sons and Lovers* (London: Penguin, 1995)

Levi, Primo, *If This Is A Man. The Truce* (London: Abacus, 1987)

Morrell, David, *Lessons from a lifetime of Writing: a novelist looks at his craft* (Cincinnati: Writer's Digest Books, 2002)

Pennebaker, James W., *Writing To Heal: A Guided Journal for Recovering from Trauma and Emotional Upheaval* (Oakland: Harbinger Publications Inc, 2004)

Pennebaker, James W., *Emotion, Disclosure & Health*, (Washington DC: American Psychological Association, 1995)

Plath, Sylvia, *The Belljar,* (London: Faber and Faber, 1963).

Rose, Gilbert, J, *Trauma and Mastery in Life and Art* (New Haven and London: Yale University Press, 1923)

Seals, Marc, 'Trauma Theory and Hemingway's Lost Paris Manuscripts', *Project MUSE: Scholarly Journals Online*: http://muse.jhu.edu/login?uri=/journals/hemingway_review/v024/24.2seals.html [accessed 12 January 2008]

Williams, Tennessee, *The Glass Menagerie* (London: Methuen Publishing Ltd, 2000)

Woolf, Virginia, *A Room of One's Own – Three Guineas* (Oxford: Oxford University Press, 1992)

Wroe, Simon, 'The Review', *The Camden New Journal* (October 2007) Available at http://www.thecnj.com/review/2007/100407/books100407_03.html [Accessed 11 January 2008]

Wyn, Nia, *Blue Sky July* (Bridgend: Seren, 2007)

Notes on Contributors

Paul Belanger has been a community literacy and arts organizer, helped develop literacy projects in the Caribbean, and has taught English in South Korea. He graduated from the University of Wisconsin and is planning to pursue his PhD in Australia. He is currently working on his first novel, *The Plague Room*, a historical rendering of an Edinburgh ghost story.

Ruth T Calway was born of a Welsh mother and English father and has divided most of her life between South Wales and the West Country, with fifteen years in Bedfordshire. She worked for many years as an arboriculturalist, gardener and plantswoman especially devoted to ancient woodland conservation. She has come to writing stories recently and sees the form as an extension of poetry, her first love.

Gavin Goodwin was born in Newport, Gwent, in 1977. On leaving school he began writing songs, and as part of the band, Terris, released an E.P. with Rough Trade in 1999 and an album with Blanco Y Negro in 2001. After his recording contract expired he spent time working in a kitchen and bar, before becoming a support worker for adults with learning disabilities. In 2007 he graduated from Cardiff University where he is about to begin work on a doctorate.

Robert D Leis was born in a village two hours west of Chicago, Illinois. His childhood was spent exploring the huge tract of wooded area behind his house. On entering high school he moved to Kenosha, Wisconsin, and attended the University of Wisconsin-Milwaukee. He taught English at a private academy in South Korea before his year in Cardiff. He has returned to South Korea and continues to teach.

Alaleh Mohajerani was born in Tehran, Iran, in 1980. She has since lived in Spain, Germany, the United States, Greece, and Wales. The pieces featured in this anthology are the opening chapters of her first novel.

Claire Morton was born in Chichester on New Year's Day 1984. She taught in Peru and travelled the world before studying English Literature at Cardiff. She is part of a close-knit family, whose love and support she could not be without. Her MA year at Cardiff has given her enough courage to embark on writing a novel. She is currently teaching in a secondary school in Devon.

William Muir was born in Glasgow in 1967. His first novel, *The 18th Pale Descendant*, was published in 2001 by Quartet Books, London. He is currently working on a new book entitled *Empire of Dirt*.

Rahul Sethi was born in New Delhi in 1983 and migrated to Canada with his parents and elder brother in 1989. He has lived in and near Toronto ever since, apart from his year in Cardiff. His first book, *From the Knotted Locks of Shiva*, was published in 2007 by Life Rattle Press, Toronto. His stories and poetry have appeared in a number of literary journals. He is an instructor for a course entitled An Introduction to Expressive Writing at the University of Toronto.

Cathy Smith sees herself as Scottish, has lived a long time in England, and is now in Wales. In her working life as an international executive she has enjoyed travelling to remote locations, and has developed a fascination with different countries and diverse cultures. She describes the year pursuing her Master's at Cardiff as the perfect transition from a globe-trotting career to a long-held dream of writing. Her current novel, *Shifting Sands*, is set in Kuwait, Kazakhstan and the U.K.

John Whittles was born in 1986 and studied English at Cardiff University, where he discovered a passion for creative writing. Influences on his work range from David Mamet to Raymond Carver, and from Cormac McCarthy to Chris Morris. In addition to writing short stories he writes for the stage, radio and the screen. In 2007 John co-wrote and directed a stage comedy that was performed by members of Cardiff's Act One drama society. He is currently writing a feature-length screenplay based on his time working in a band rehearsal rooms.

Nia Wyn is from North Wales and lives in Cardiff. She is an award-winning journalist. Her book *Blue Sky July*, a love story charting her experiences with her son Joe, was published by Seren and serialised in *The Guardian*, *The Daily Mail*, and on Radio 4. Penguin UK and US bought the paperback rights. *Blue Sky July* has been released in Australia and America, with launches in South Africa, Italy and Holland due in 2009 and was the runner-up in the 2008 Wales Book of the Year award.

John Freeman has taught English Literature at Cardiff University since 1972, and Creative Writing since its inauguration as an option in the BA course there in 1983. He has published articles on Shelley, a book of essays on modern poets, and several collections of his own poetry of which the most recent is *A Suite For Summer*, Worple Press, 2007.